YOU KNOW HIM . . .

You've seen his expressive face a thousand times: as Dr. Huxtable on the top-rated *The Cosby Show*; picking up gold records and Grammy Awards for his comedy albums; receiving three Emmys in a row for best actor; knocking them dead on *The Tonight Show*

BUT THERE'S MORE . . .

Bill Cosby—For Real tells you all about this versatile talent's incredible life and delves into his serious side, exploring his thoughts on education, success, and family life. So learn the whole fantastic Cosby story—as it's never been told before.

D0101236

Bill Cosby —For Real

CAROLINE LATHAM

TOR

A TOM DOHERTY ASSOCIATES BOOK

BILL COSBY—FOR REAL

Copyright © 1985 by Caroline Latham

First printing: November 1985

A TOR Book

Published by Tom Doherty Associates
49 West 24 Street
New York, N.Y. 10010

ISBN: 0-812-59450-9
CAN. ED.: 0-812-59451-7

Printed in the United States of America

0   9   8   7   6   5   4   3

Table of Contents

BILL COSBY—FOR REAL

still the little boy who's afraid his father is going to catch him in some mischief, who's indignant about having to share his bed with his brother, who lies awake worrying about what horrible creature might be hiding in his closet.

And he knows that the rest of us have a child like that inside us, too. He is successful precisely because his famed comedy routines speak to that child in each member of his audience. When he's at his best, the child in all of us answers him back, in laughter and appreciation and a feeling of warmth that few other comics have managed to evoke.

As a result of his ability to keep the child in himself alive and well, Bill Cosby's career has already lasted nearly twenty-five years, and it's never been healthier than it is today. Perhaps because his humor comes from basic human relationships rather than trendy one-liners, he has proved to be one of the most durable entertainers in the business. His new television series, *The Cosby Show*, of which he is both star and coproducer (as well as the educational consultant) was the top-ranked new show of the 1984–85 season, reaching number one in the weekly ratings. It was promptly renewed and proved to hold up as well in its second season as it did in its first. Bill was nominated for an Emmy for his work on the show, and most insiders agree he would have won, but he refused to compete with his fellow professionals and asked to be withdrawn from the list of nominees. Although the schedule demands of a weekly series have kept him off the club circuit the last few years, he could be earning at least $50,000 a night if he were willing to go to work in Vegas or Tahoe or Atlantic City.

His record albums are still steady sellers, and some of his old routines are such classics that they turn up today on top 40 radio stations. He was recently featured on the cover of *US* magazine and in 1986 *Cosby on Fatherhood*, which he is writing, will be published. Even his commercials are a success. The ones he recently made for Coke remain daunting competition for Pepsi, even though they have tried to counter with Michael Jackson, Lionel Richie, and Geraldine Ferraro. As one critic noted, what Bill Cosby is really selling, rather than Jell-O or Coke, is reassurance.

His career has been just as successful artistically as it has financially, an uncommon achievement for any prime-time entertainer. Critics all love his new show, calling it a warm, sensitive, and funny portrayal of family life that is, nevertheless, dead accurate in its depiction of the relationship between parents and children. They especially praise the fact that the humor in the show arises from character, rather than manufactured comedy routines; the show doesn't have gags, it's just *funny*. It is evident that the years of experience since his first hit TV series (*I Spy*, back in the late sixties) have taught him to use the intimacy of the television screen to his advantage. Even people who don't like ''family entertainment'' are watching

The Cosby Show because Bill is just too good to miss.

The grown-up in Bill Cosby must be delighted by all this success. Yet the wise child in him is fighting against taking it all too seriously. He's still ready to try something new, to take a gamble, to fail right out there in public. His love of music has led him to put out a couple of records on which he sings himself. He's also been active in the world of jazz, recently acting as producer for a night of jazz during New York's Kool Jazz Festival. In 1983, he took the risk of putting together a Broadway show that consisted of nothing but himself and Sammy Davis, Jr., telling jokes and singing and dancing.

Sometimes Bill's inner promptings lead him even further afield. There have been periods in the course of his successful career when he has considered limiting his professional activities to real children. At one time, he thought seriously about quitting show business to go into teaching. But a good classroom teacher can only reach a few hundred students in the course of an entire career, whereas a superstar like Bill Cosby can reach millions of kids. Although he did earn a Ph.D. in education from the University of Massachusetts, he decided against becoming a classroom teacher. But that doesn't mean he has abandoned his goal of teaching children; he simply decided to do it in a different way—through films and Saturday morning cartoons and a TV series that is scheduled early enough in the evening for kids to be able to watch. His intention was stated explicitly at the start of each episode of the cartoon show he created, *The New Fat Albert Show*, when he looked into the camera and addressed his viewers: "Here's Bill Cosby coming at you with music and fun, and if you're not careful, you may learn something."

Many parents of young children feel that Bill Cosby is not only a good teacher, but also a valuable role model. He is obviously a devoted family man: a good husband, father, and son. He is a hard worker and a reliable one, too, always on time and always professionally prepared for his job. He doesn't drink or take drugs, and that's not just P.R. hype—it's really true. His only vices are huge Cuban cigars and fast sports cars (although these days he is likely to be driving *within* the speed limit). He respects his mother and loves his wife and remains loyal to old friends. These are all virtues that one doesn't expect to find in a superstar who has the money and opportunity to do just about anything. It's nothing short of heartwarming.

Yet there are rumors that Bill Cosby is not always the warm and wonderful human being that is projected on our television screens. Some journalists have reported that he can be very uncooperative about interviews, on occasion even downright hostile in response to personal questions. Fans have sometimes been disappointed by his refusal to sign autographs and pose for snapshots. A certain segment of the black community has complained that he has not done enough to help others of his race. And all of us who follow his career

Chapter Two

"I Started Out As a Child"

To get myself across and to be an important person, I made people laugh. Through humor, I gained acceptance.

What can young people, black and white, do to help improve relations? They can try to be as fair with each other as is humanly possible. And that's the important thing: fair. Not what they think is fair, but what *is* fair.

BILL COSBY'S CHILDHOOD is already legendary. So much of his comedy material has been built around the events of his childhood that it seems we have virtually lived through it with him. We know all about the fights with his brother Russell, the improvised alibis to his father, the friends in the neighborhood. Like every artist, he takes the raw material of life and turns it into a finished work of art. The record shows that the raw material of his own life was somewhat darker than his warm recollections suggest.

William Henry Cosby, Jr., was born on July 12, 1937, around three o'clock in the morning, in Germantown Hospital, North Philadelphia. He was the first son of Anna and William Cosby, childhood sweethearts in Virginia who married and migrated north in the depths of the Depression. The Cosbys lived in a small apartment in Philadelphia's black neighborhood, and as they began to create a family, they also were creating a life for that family that was, if not prosperous, at least comfortable. Bill's father worked at a variety of jobs—anything that called for a hard worker with no particular skills—and he did his best, for a few years, to act as head of the household and sole wage earner.

The family expanded. Bill had three younger brothers. James was two years younger; then came Russell, about five and a half years younger; then Robert, nearly nine years younger. Anna Cosby was a full-time mother during those early years, tending her family of growing boys. But she was unable to prevent James, a sickly child, from contracting rheumatic fever; he died from it when he was just six years old.

James's death was one of those knocks of fate that can change everything. Within months of that event, Bill's father gave up on the increasingly difficult struggle to earn a living in Philadelphia. He came home one day and announced he had joined the navy as a ship's steward. That decision effectively removed William Cosby from the family. He told Bill at the time, "This means you're the man of the house," and he was right. Although he did send some of his pay home to help support his family, he was no longer a presence in the house. Eventually, he and Bill's mother turned this de facto separation into a legal one and got divorced.

By this point the Cosby family had moved from a middle-class neighborhood to one of Philadelphia's low-income housing projects. Their circumstances were decent, but never more than that. The money that William Cosby sent home wasn't enough to pay the rent and buy food and clothes for Anna and her three sons, so she took a job as a maid, earning about $8 a day. Occasionally a lack of steady work would put the family on welfare for a brief period, but for the most part, they could take care of themselves. The boys all helped out by taking odd jobs around the neighborhood as soon as they were old enough.

With his father away, and his mother out working all day, young Bill became the man of the house—and, to some extent, the woman, too. He was responsible for the care of his younger brothers after school, and he did some of the cooking and cleaning. His specialties in the kitchen were spaghetti, popcorn, and waffles—just the sort of well-balanced diet a ten-year-old kid would think up! Bill brought a touch of imagination to the dishes he cooked. He recalls the stage during which he always added food coloring to the waffles. "I liked purple waffles, green, orange, red waffles. I loved them, and I couldn't understand why my mother never dug them."

Bill shared a room with his brothers, and yes, he really did have to sleep with Russell. Like all brothers, they sometimes fought. Bill recalls, "We had our little fights and our differences about things like who had a bigger piece of pie, who ate two pieces of cake, and later on, about property."

As a comedian, Bill drew on his memories of those universal childhood experiences of fighting with his brothers, trying to conceal his misbehavior from his parents, pretending to be more grown-up than he really was. One of his funniest routines is about the feigned casualness of a kindergartner leaving his mother for the first time. But what Bill doesn't like to talk about are his specific experiences growing up poor and black . . . and eventually fatherless. Things like the year the family had no Christmas tree, how hard his mother always had to work, and the realization that there would never be money for things like comic books or clothes that were in style are taboo subjects. Like a magician misdirecting our attention, Bill Cosby talks about the warm and funny events of his childhood to hide the real pain.

Bill's comedy routines about his childhood often feature his father and, in fact, generally portray him in a sympathetic light as a hardworking and long-suffering man who is simply trying to keep his imaginative and unruly children under control. But the grown-up Bill Cosby rarely talks about his father. It doesn't take psychiatric training to guess that the nine-year-old Bill felt his father's departure for the navy was really a desertion, one that he still finds hard to forgive. Yet if thinking about his father brings some measure of pain, he understands enough about his father's reasons for leaving to prevent real bitterness. As Bill once told a reporter inquiring about his childhood, "I believe in learning from your mistakes and not becoming bitter. Unhappiness should make a person appreciate happiness more, and hard times should give a person backbone and moral strength."

There's certainly no mistaking the love and admiration Bill Cosby feels for his mother. She was the one who held the family together all those years, doing whatever she had to do to accomplish the goal. She was the one who inculcated a sense of right and wrong in the boys, in a gentle but insistent way. Bill and his brothers recall that she rarely spanked or punished them. But when they did something she thought was wrong, she always began to cry. Says Bill, "Her tears alone would shake us up. She'd start crying and you'd start crying." In one of his early comedy routines, Bill teased his mother about her inclination toward tears. "Mom was groovy—she'd cry over anything. Find a piece of wood. 'That's beautiful,' she'd cry."

Bill's mother had a deep belief in the value of education, and she encouraged her sons to do their best in school. She also tried at home to give them an interest in reading, and it became a family ritual for her to read aloud to the boys every night before they went to bed. She favored the Bible and Mark Twain, and Bill says he still remembers being frightened by some of the adventures of Huck Finn.

His mother was also one of Bill's earliest audiences. He once explained how he had started his comedy career. "I'm a con man. That's how I started out to be a comedian. . . . You start out at about three or four, conning your mother out of a cookie. You know that she'll say 'no' the first time you ask, but you also know that if you can get her to laughing, you can get around her." Bill learned to amuse his mother by telling her and his brothers funny versions of the things that happened to them in everyday life. His brother Robert remembers, "Bill could turn painful situations around and make them funny. You laughed to keep from crying." That was a talent that helped the Cosby family through some difficult years.

Bill carried his talent for making people laugh to school, too. He later explained, "I found I could make people laugh, and I enjoyed doing it. I thought that if people laughed at what you said, that meant they liked you. Telling funny stories became, for me, a way of making friends." But he had other ways of making friends. He was a well-coordinated boy with a lot of athletic ability, and "Shorty," as he was sometimes jokingly called, spent a lot of his free time playing baseball, basketball, and football. These games took place not in a green park or open field, but right on the streets of North Philadelphia. One of Bill's funniest routines is about the way he and his friends played football, with the quarterback barking out instructions for people to cut behind the black Chevy, wait in someone's living room, and get on a moving bus to catch a pass when the doors opened two blocks down the street.

By participating in sports, Bill managed to avoid the trouble so many boys from poor urban neighborhoods often fall into. He played on teams sponsored by the Police Athletic League and won local recognition for his pitching, his running, and his high jumping. His ability to tell funny stories and jokes at school also helped him achieve the recognition that some kids have to search for in less socially acceptable ways.

He was frequently cast in school plays and, for the most part, encouraged by his teachers to develop his fledgling performing talents. They did try to draw the line about his using them in the classroom, however, and Bill's fifth grade teacher wrote impatiently on his report card, "In this classroom there is one comedian, and it is I. If you want to be one, grow up, get your own stage, and get paid for it." Obviously a good piece of advice. . . .

One other thing that kept Bill Cosby from getting mixed up in the petty crime that flourished in his neighborhood was his desire to make his mother proud of him. He says matter-of-factly, "The thing that always turned me around and kept me from taking a pistol and holding up a store or jumping in and beating some old person on the street was that I could go to jail, and this would bring a great amount of shame on my mother. . . ."

But don't get the idea that "Cool Cos" was a goody-goody. He goofed off in class, didn't study, and never turned in any homework, so his grades were terrible. He often disrupted the entire class with his clowning, to the great annoyance of his teachers. He got out of some of his scrapes by signing his mother's name on papers she'd never seen. He forged her signature on a couple of bad report cards, and he also whipped up a funny letter that was supposedly from her to the collection department of a company that was trying to get Bill to pay for some expensive body-building equipment he had ordered. In his persona of Mrs. Cosby, Bill wrote to the company, "William is only eight years old and he's crazy, so don't send any more stuff to him."

When Bill graduated from elementary school, his favorite teacher told him, "You're a very intelligent young man, but you should be working at it." Bill did try hard when he was in her class, but he just wasn't ready to listen to such good advice. "I refused to accept the responsibility. I don't know what I even had in mind; it wasn't that I was going to be a professional football player or professional baseball player, or an artist or a drummer—it's just that I wanted to play."

And, of course, Bill Cosby's version of play was later to become famous, as part of his classic comedy routines about his childhood. When he told us about Fat Albert and Crying Charlie and Weird Harold and all the other kids in the neighborhood, we cracked up because we knew those very same kids, even if we called them by different names. The jokes in the classroom, the problems with the principal, the games after school, the complicated system of friendships and rivalries—

these subjects provided the basis of Bill Cosby's comedy, and he really tells it like it is. Although he is reminiscing about a particular place and time—a black neighborhood in North Philadelphia in the 1950s—his observations hold true for other times and other places. They focus on archetypal experiences of growing up.

Yet Bill Cosby was too smart and too observant not to realize that some experiences were different for him and his friends, because they were poor and black. In a funny piece he wrote for *Ebony* in 1974, he alluded to some of those differences. He tells the story of the exciting time that Frankenstein and Dracula were scheduled to appear live at his neighborhood movie theater. He says, "The feeling of the whole neighborhood was that we didn't believe it. Guys were walking around asking, 'Why should Frankenstein come to the Booker Movie when he could be downtown making a lot of money?' Nobody thought, 'My, how wonderful, Frankenstein is coming to the Booker Movie.' The people started putting themselves down. 'Why is he coming to see us?' They weren't scared of him. They just wanted to know how come such a great celebrity was coming to their theater. They were thinking, 'First of all, the seats are all ripped up and people drink wine in the movie and throw popcorn and bring sandwiches and yell at the screen.' "

However funny life in Bill Cosby's neighborhood could sometimes be, it was, nevertheless, a life of limited options, of restricted opportunities.

Bill had already found out just how difficult it was to find work when you didn't have an education, and just how boring that work could be. He had worked as a shoeshine boy and a grocery delivery boy to bring in a little extra money for the family and he had not liked the prospect of a lifetime of jobs like those. His mother kept telling him that the way out was education. So far Bill had found little interest in the classroom, but maybe things could change.

At that time, the best school in the Philadelphia system—in fact, one of the top ten in the nation—was Central High School. Central, a school for boys only, accepted boys from all over the city based on a qualifying exam and their past records. Although Bill had poor grades, he got good recommendations from his teachers, and he passed the exam. Moreover, his participation in sports gave him a quality much admired in admissions offices everywhere—he was "well rounded." So Bill won a place at Central High. The school itself was lovely, with a big rolling campus and well-equipped classrooms—very much like a college rather than a public high school. About 95 percent of Central High graduates went on to college, and by and large, the students were academically ambitious boys who worked hard at their studies. Many were the sons of first-generation Central High graduates and had as many educational advantages at home as they did in school. Perhaps the best way to sum up the boys who attended Central High is to cite the ironic cheer used by other schools when competitors from Central took the field: "Knit one, purl two, Central High, woo woo."

As at his other schools, Bill Cosby was popular at Central High. He was on the student council, he was the class clown, he was very good at sports. But he failed to take advantage of the educational advantages the school offered. Dr. William H. Cosby, Jr., with a Ph.D. in education, could probably explain the reasons why. Bill never had been a diligent student, and being at Central High didn't change that fact. Sports meant more to him than studies. In junior high, he had been captain of the tumbling team, and he continued to play baseball and basketball in community-sponsored leagues. He knew he didn't want to live in North Philadelphia all his life, and he thought sports would be his ticket out of the neighborhood. Moreover, he really didn't fit in academically in a school where kids were studying Latin and calculus. He simply didn't have the background, in his previous educational experience or at home, to take to it easily. No doubt he could have done well if he had really concentrated on his studies, but he wasn't motivated to spend hours at home alone in the evening doing his homework. He preferred to spend the time with his friends.

As a result, he failed nearly every one of his courses in tenth grade. When he went back to repeat them the following year, he was still having trouble. Eventually, he decided that it was the better part of wisdom to transfer back to his neighborhood high school.

He was certainly happier at Germantown High. He was the captain of both the football and the track team, distinguishing himself as a running back and as a high jumper. And this school also had girls. He says he didn't really go out on dates in high school because he didn't have the money for it. But he went to parties and school dances and other gatherings. "You could dress up any old way to go to a party, 'cause they turn the lights out and they can't see your pants don't match." At least at Germantown High he was having fun. But he really wasn't doing much better academically, despite the easier work. The truth of the matter was that in his teens Bill Cosby was just not cut out to be a student.

By the time Bill was nineteen, he still hadn't finished high school, and things weren't much fun anymore. He was too old to be allowed to compete in the city track meets, and he was beginning to feel like many of his football teammates were "just kids." He had long since given up the hope of achieving any academic distinction, and finally he also gave up the hope of getting a high school diploma. He dropped out of school in 1956.

He tried looking for work in Philadelphia and was briefly employed in a muffler plant and a shoe repair store (the owner asked him to leave when he found Bill amusing himself by nailing high heels on men's shoes). Discouraged about his future, Bill did what many other young men in the same situation have done: he enlisted in the navy. Bill signed up for a four-year hitch. That period seems to have been a turning point for him. It was while he was in the navy that he finally realized it was time to grow up.

Bill profited in many ways from the time he spent in the service. He had the chance to compete for the navy as a high jumper and set several new records at the meets he attended. He was trained as a physical therapist and found that the ability to help other people was rewarding. He got the chance to see a little bit of the world, since he was stationed in Newfoundland, Argentina, and Cuba, as well as at naval hospitals in and around Philadelphia. Bill says he is convinced he would have had a great career as a physical therapist, and he's probably right. While he helped patients relearn basic skills such as walking and feeding themselves, he also made them laugh. He still had the ability he had acquired as a child to look trouble right in the face and crack a joke about it, and that must have been a big help to the disabled men he worked with.

Although the navy brought Bill certain satisfactions, he decided against making it his career. "I didn't like the guys who were bossing me around, telling me to clean up any old thing any old time for no reason—'Do it because I said to do it.' I knew I didn't want to stay in the service. Now the only way you can get out of it is to get yourself an education, unless you want to go back to civilian life and wait on tables . . . not even wait on tables, but just take glasses off, which I knew was where I was headed.''

So at the age of twenty-three Bill Cosby had come full circle. It was time to go back to school—and this time he was serious about it.

Chapter Three

Bill Cosby Discovers He *Is* a Very Funny Fellow

I'm one of the lucky ones. But I don't intend to rely on luck. That's why I'm out there hustling as hard as I am.

FOR BILL COSBY, the first step in going to college was to finish high school. While still in the navy, he arranged to take a high school equivalency test. Thanks to his native intelligence, and the general experience he had acquired in the previous four years, he passed easily.

The next step was somewhat more difficult. Not only did he have to get accepted at a college, he had to win a scholarship, since there was no way he could manage to pay the tuition himself. By living at home he could hold down the costs of room and board, and his mother, who was pleased to see her son interested in attending college at last, was willing to do all she could to help. All Bill had to do was find help with his tuition. He concentrated his attention on the Philadelphia area.

At a track meet he attended as a member of the navy team, he introduced himself to the coach of the Temple University track team. First, Bill told some jokes that left the poor coach laughing helplessly, and then he produced evidence of his good record in track, including his high jump of six feet five inches, at that time a significant achievement. The result was that in September 1960, Bill Cosby entered his freshman year at Temple with a full-tuition athletic scholarship.

The Bill Cosby who enrolled at Temple was a very different person from the one who had dropped out of high school four years earlier. He was serious now about doing well academically and ready and willing to put in the work that it required. Although he had decided to become a physical education major, he had to take the required freshman courses, such as English Composition and Introductory Biology. The amount of time he had to spend at the athletic pursuits that were the basis of his scholarship left him little time for studying; nevertheless, his grades in his freshman year were quite good—nearly good enough to get him on the honor roll. He planned to graduate in four years and go to work as a physical education teacher.

Meanwhile, he was one of Temple's outstanding athletes. He played on the freshman basketball team, although his height was just a shade under six feet, short for the sport. He also played on the varsity football team, admittedly one of the weaker teams in its conference. Bill recalls it as "the nut squad" and claims, "We used to run around with our helmets on sideways, looking through the earholes." His coach remembers him as "a fiery competitor who wanted to excel." Because of his size and aggressiveness Bill played fullback, but he wasn't too happy with that position. He wanted to be a halfback. However, he had the discipline of a team player and did his best.

It was the track team that really brought out his enthusiasm. His best event was the high jump, but he also competed in the hurdles, the hop-skip-jump, the discus and javelin throws, and the shot put. He might have been a very good decathlon competitor if the training and support had been available to him. As it was, he was usually one of the top scorers for his team at track meets, and his coach, Gavin White, says he was a tremendous athlete.

One of Bill's outstanding personality traits in college, as now, was his ability to see the funny side of everything. He loves to tell the story about the time he was running anchor for Temple's team at a big Philadelphia track meet that had attracted an audience of seventy thousand. "We're all lined up there, with itchy feet, waiting to get the baton and take off. But as my man gets near to the passing point, the baton hits his leg and flies up in the air. What does this cat do? He just starts to laugh. All the other anchor men are off and running, and I'm standing there waiting for this nut to stop laughing, pick up the baton, and give it to me. Finally, he retrieves it and walks over to me with the damn thing. *Walks!* I took it and bopped him right on the head with it, which is when the fans began screaming with laughter. But that's not the end of it. Old Cosby's a team player to the end, and I take off after those runners like a madman. I'm running and running, and passing one guy and then another, and then I get what you call rigor mortis if you're a runner. It's from the effort. First my face muscles freeze and then my chest, then my legs. I fall down, a beaten man if ever there was one, and while I'm down, the cat I had hit over the head comes up, takes the baton, and bops me back with it. I couldn't dream up a routine that funny.''

During his sophomore year at Temple, Bill continued to do well in the classroom, and track remained a bright spot. But when it came to the football team, he found he was spending most of his time on the bench. As he put it, ironically, ''It got to be an awfully long season.'' The best thing about football was the friendships he made with other players. With his sense of humor and his storytelling ability, Bill was usually the center of attention. Even off the field, his most frequent companions were other athletes; he was what might be called a man's man. But that's not to say he neglected the ladies. He went out with a number of different girls, explaining, ''Cos is beautiful. All the women should have a chance to share Cos.''

One other thing Bill did that sophomore year was look for a part-time job to provide necessary pocket money while he was in school. He had a friend who owned a little bar called The Underground, located in a basement. The friend gave Bill the job of tending bar for $5 a night plus tips. Bill soon learned that the best way to get good tips was to make his customers laugh. The bar actually had a resident comedian, and every now and again, when he didn't show up or had had too many drinks on the house, Bill was asked to take over his spot. Says Bill, "It got to be a thing. That comedian was no drunker than I was most of the time, but I got twenty-five bucks whenever I went on, and he knew I needed the loot, so he'd just kind of not show up now and then."

The fame of the funny bartender began to spread around Philadelphia. The result was that Bill was offered a job next door at The Cellar, a club owned by the same management as the bar, at $12.50 a night as a stand-up comic—well, almost standing up. In actual fact, the ceiling was too low for Bill to be able to stand up straight while he did his act. The choices were to crouch like a boxer jabbing an opponent or to put a chair on a low table and become a sit-down comic. Onstage, Bill acted very much the way he did with his friends on the football and track teams. He gave the impression of a good friend who was just telling a few funny stories to pass the time, and he was an immediate success.

Bill turned to a cousin, Del Shields, for advice on how to capitalize on this local success. Del had a radio show on a Philadelphia FM station, and he knew a little bit about the clubs that hired live performers. With his guidance, Bill managed to get more local bookings, and it gave him the opportunity to polish up some of his routines. He tried writing his comedy material with a partner, an experiment that lasted just two weeks. According to Bill, the partner had the deplorable habit of waiting until two minutes before Bill was scheduled to go out in front of the audience and then telling Bill he didn't really think the material was funny. Like many other young comedians, Bill also stole some material from more famous performers. He listened to Mel Brooks, Jonathan Winters, Bob Newhart, and Lenny Bruce and took the routines that appealed to him. It was a way of mastering timing, delivery, and stage presence without having to worry about the quality of the material.

In the late spring of 1962, Bill's local success made him decide to seek work in New York. He got a booking to appear at the Gaslight Cafe, then a famous coffeehouse in Greenwich Village. He was paid $60 a week and given a free room. He managed to juggle his schedule so that he was able to work there at night and finish up his classes at Temple during the day. By summertime, he was able to give his full time and attention to his comedy work and was such a hit that the club offered him an extended engagement at the princely salary of $175 a week—and this time the room he was given even had plumbing! Bill says of his employment by the Gaslight, ''The idea was to break the monotony of the folksingers. That was my job. In time, I became monotonous in my own right.''

Bill's first big break came that summer, when reviewer Paul Gardner of *The New York Times* went to the Gaslight to take in Bill's act. He wrote a glowing report, published on June 25, 1962: ''Mr. Cosby writes his own material. Although his output thus far is limited, his viewpoint is fresh, slightly ironic, and his best quips are extremely funny. He is a man of considerable promise who should keep Gaslight habitués laughing between sips of espresso.'' Gardner also commented, ''Mr. Cosby speaks slowly, carefully, almost shyly. He wears a plaid sport coat, dark slacks, a conservative tie, and a button-down shirt. While sitting on a straw bar stool on the tiny Gaslight stage, he seems to be waiting for a young girl to take to the senior prom.'' The three-column review was accompanied by a picture of Bill mugging with that magically rubbery face.

It would be an exaggeration to say that one review in the *Times* made Bill Cosby a star overnight. But the review did attract audiences at a very early stage of his career, and that had an immediate effect on the bookings he was able to get. By the end of the summer, he was offered a stint at the Gate of Horn in Chicago for $200 a week; in 1962, that was decent money for a single man of twenty-five. But it raised a problem about finishing college.

When his gig in Chicago was over, he had to report immediately for preseason football practice.

According to one source, Bill was out of condition
and fifteen pounds overweight, because he had
done nothing all summer but stand up in a dark
room at night telling jokes. He tried to go on with
his academic responsibilities until the schedule pressures became unsolvable. That fall he had a chance
to play Philadelphia's Town Hall for $250 a night,
but taking the job would mean he couldn't travel
with the football team to Toledo on Friday night
for their game the next afternoon. Bill asked the
coach for permission to travel there on his own
Saturday morning, but the coach refused. Either
Bill behaved like all the other team members, or
he would be off the team. And, of course, if Bill
was off the team, he would lose his scholarship at
Temple. Even if he could find a solution to that
particular problem, Bill was already aware that his
work as a comedian would conflict with the time
he needed for his studies to finish up the last two
years of college; his grades were starting to slide.
It seemed clear that he was now going to have to
choose one or the other.

It must have been a very difficult decision for
Bill Cosby. All his life, his mother had stressed
the value of education as the key to a better life.
Moreover, he had worked hard to get back on the
track after his poor record in high school, and he
hated to throw all that effort away before he earned
his college degree. He knew how much he had
grown to regret his earlier decision to drop out of
high school, and he might feel exactly the same in
a few years if he dropped out of college now. On

the other hand, his career as a comedian was moving faster than he ever could have hoped. He had future bookings lined up, and his fees were increasing steadily. Did it make any sense to turn his back on a thriving career in show business just to get a college degree? After all, he was already earning as much as he could hope to make as a teacher once he was out of school.

In the end he opted for show business, and in November 1962, he dropped out of Temple. He told a friend at the time that his ambition was to earn $300 a week for ten years, and then quit and fulfill his original dream: finish school and be a phys ed teacher. But it quickly became apparent that his ambitions were far too modest. He was, in fact, on his way to stardom.

In early 1963, Bill started to appear all over the country. He was at the Shadows Club and the Shoreham Hotel in Washington; at the Fifth Peg in Toronto; at the hungry i in San Francisco. Everywhere he went, he got good reviews. Perhaps even more important, he began to meet people who took an interest in his career. He got acquainted with fellow comedians such as Sandy Baron, George Carlin, Richard Pryor—all playing somewhat the same circuit. He got to know the club owners, who understood that he could pull in a large audience. And he got to know some of his fans.

One of them was Roy Silver. Roy was a few years older than Bill and lived in the Village, where he had a chance to meet most of the comics who performed there. Roy had worked in the office that had managed the career of Bob Dylan, and after a falling-out with his boss that led to his firing, Roy wanted to make a career managing talent on his own. Roy had lots of ideas about how a good comic could reach the top. He explained, "I was thinking that TV was the place for comedians, and yet comedians who depend strictly on material weren't making it there. Jack Benny, Bob Hope, Jackie Gleason—they were all great TV performers because of their personalities. It hardly mattered whether they had jokes, or what the jokes were. People laughed just when they saw them. Yet, here is this guy Bill, who can break you up just looking at you, and he's getting up on the floor and trying to make it by telling jokes. It was all wrong."

Roy Silver became Bill Cosby's manager. He went to all Bill's performances, tape-recorded the shows, and then sat down with Bill afterward to analyze what had worked and what hadn't. He helped Bill make the transition from being a fellow who was always able to make his friends laugh to being a professional comic. Whatever the value of his insights, he made the important contribution of taking Bill seriously as a potential star. And he made Bill look at himself in the same way. So Bill began polishing his routines, perfecting his comic persona. He really worked at his profession—as even the most talented must do if they are to succeed.

*   *   *

Roy Silver helped Bill Cosby see what his future could be. Determinedly ambitious, Roy was thinking far beyond the possibility of Bill earning a mere $300 a week or making a career out of nothing but traveling from one club to another. He was looking for ways Bill Cosby could get into the big time. And he was convinced that TV was one of those ways. As soon as Bill's fee began to go up, Roy talked him into spending the money on hiring a press agent. Says Roy, "He had one job, to plant items in columns that Bill Cosby was the first Negro ever being considered for a TV series. Bill *who*? He was beginning to make his move a little, working good rooms like Mr. Kelly's in Chicago, but nobody had ever heard of him really. But slowly, slowly, we got maybe seventy-five mentions, and it began to seep into people's minds in places like William Morris [one of the country's top talent agencies], and suddenly it wasn't a completely crazy notion anymore. Bill was feasible."

Meanwhile, Bill was also working hard in comedy rooms all over the country. His regular appearances and good reviews made Warner Brothers think about signing him up to do a comedy album, and it was recorded live at The Bitter End in late 1963. The title of the album was *Bill Cosby Is a Very Funny Fellow . . . Right!* and it was produced by Roy Silver and Allan Sherman, who was a pretty funny fellow in his own right. He parodied folk songs to devastating effect and had had a big hit the year before with his ballad of a kid who wants to come home from summer camp.

Sherman immediately became one of Bill Cosby's foremost fans. In the notes on the back of the record, he wrote, "Bill Cosby has a wonderful, cockeyed, fresh sense of humor. He is so good that what he has is more than talent; he has the gift of comedy. He has something that makes you feel delight when you're with him. . . . Bill Cosby would be funny if he were green or purple or chartreuse. He's funny because he can feel for people—and he can communicate that feeling. . . . I wish I could look at your face when you first hear this album. I wish I could be with you when you first discover Bill Cosby. I don't know who you are; all I know is that you are one of the millions of people who buy records and who made my life so crazy and wonderful during the last year. I want to return the favor. That's why I'm so proud and happy for the chance to introduce you to Bill Cosby. It isn't every day that we come into contact with greatness. The day you first listen to this album will be one of those days for you."

That's some promo! And the best part was that Allan Sherman meant every word he said. He *was* eager to introduce Bill Cosby to the American public . . . and soon he got another chance. Near the end of 1963, Allan was asked to fill in as a guest host for Johnny Carson. One of the guests he invited to appear on the show was Bill Cosby. Sherman had to fight the show's producer, who was dubious about a black comic, but he won, and he even asked Bill to join him on the couch after his bit. At that time, lesser performers were dismissed as soon as they entertained, but stars were invited to stay and chat.

Allan's gamble worked. Bill's spot on the show was a success, and his career as a star was launched. He was able to ask $1,500 a night on the strength of his first television appearance. His first album did amazingly well, spending 128 weeks on the charts and eventually rising as far as number twenty-one. To top it off, the album won a Grammy Award. Warner Brothers quickly signed him up to make a second album, released late in 1964, called *I Started Out As a Child*. That album was recorded live at Mr. Kelly's in Chicago, and once again it was produced by Allan Sherman and Roy Silver. It was just as successful as the first album and, like it, earned more than $1 million in sales. The second album also won a Grammy Award for Best Comedy Album of the Year. That led to more appearances in clubs and on television. Bill did *The Jack Paar Show* and *The Garry Moore Show*, he played the Flamingo Hotel in Vegas and Harrah's in Tahoe, and he even appeared in front of President Lyndon B. Johnson. Meanwhile, his fee kept going up and up, and his fame as a funny story-teller continued to spread.

Chapter Four

The Root of
Cosby Comedy

It would be so easy to go out and plant my feet and do racial jokes. It's built in for you—the back of the bus, the front of the bus, everything having to do with the suppression of the black man. But it's not my purpose to make people feel guilty about the treatment of the black man by bigots.

BILL COSBY LIKED to tell funny stories.

That's the way he entertained his younger brothers and made his hardworking mother smile at the end of the day. That's the way he achieved popularity in school, and the way he got along with his fellow students. That's the way he brightened up the hours spent in training and preseason practice with other athletes. And, one suspects, that's the way he dealt with the hurts and unhappiness of his young life.

Bill made his debut as a comedian by telling funny stories to his customers at the bar to get bigger tips. But when he found himself out on the stage alone, expected to be funny, he began to have doubts about relying on funny stories alone. He thought he needed "material"—a string of jokes, the one-liners that most people think of as the comedian's stock-in-trade. Bill once looked back and assessed some of the problems he had in the early days. "At that time, there was no Fat Albert or any of the other characters. I was basically doing sociopolitical material, learning to be a stand-up comic. You cannot learn to do that at home. . . ."

But Bill really didn't need to get up and fire one-liners at the audience. He had the kind of likability that would make audiences go along with him on practically anything. That was something that was noticed by a friend from Central High, Eddie Weinberger, who later went on to write for some of television's funniest comedy series, including *The Cosby Show*. Weinberger recalls seeing Bill at the Gaslight. "He was rambling and had no identity and had nothing going except this one quality of being likable on stage."

Weinberger instinctively understood the solution. "Bill didn't need someone to think for him, only to listen to him. That was the way to write for him. He needed to go back into his childhood and exaggerate. He had total recall. He could remember his first date, his first shave. It was like an analysis. And these things became the best part of his act because they were his own. Jonathan Winters could do voices. Dick Gregory could do race jokes. But only Bill could do his own childhood."

Interestingly, that was the very same advice he got from his grandfather. Samuel Cosby, then in his eighties, listened to Bill telling the jokes that were part of his early act. After a long silence he said tactfully, "Why don't you tell the story about when you and your brothers . . ." Roy Silver had already arrived at the same conclusion, and he worked with Bill to help him develop his stories, acting as the listener who could draw them out of Bill. Bill was then able to do the polishing that turned them into audience favorites.

It actually took a number of years for Bill to fully tap the humor implicit in his storytelling abilities. His first album, *Bill Cosby Is a Very Funny Fellow . . . Right!*, contains not a single cut based on Bill's own childhood. He does his famous Noah routine, he talks about the nuts in the New York subway, he parodies athletes doing commercials, he puzzles over the reasons why women always go to the ladies' room in groups, and he laughs at Superman, locker-room pep talks, and other staples of American culture. But he says nothing personal.

It's not until the second album that stories based on his own life begin to show up. He talks about the first kid in the neighborhood to own a pair of sneakers, and he does his very funny routine about the way football is played in the streets of Philadelphia. His father puts in his first appearance as "the Giant," and Bill's brothers and mother enter the cast of supporting characters. Here Bill Cosby is really beginning to hit his stride.

It may come as a surprise to many people to learn that in his early days, Bill Cosby did a number of jokes on racial themes. He had a bit about the first black president complaining that a lot of "for sale" signs were suddenly going up on the White House block, adding, "I used to live in a nice neighborhood . . . then two white families moved in." He even threatened his audience by saying, "You'd better laugh. I've got a club that's the opposite of the Ku Klux Klan."

But Bill himself was uneasy about this form of humor. He later remarked, "When I told racial jokes, the Negroes looked at the whites, the whites looked at the Negroes, and no one laughed—until I brought them together, and then I had to tell the jokes all over again." He concluded, "The whole question about Negro comics is this: If they colored us white, would we still be funny?"

The inclusion of overtly racial material made Bill seem indistinguishable from other black comedians. As Roy Silver put it, "It was still largely a racial act in the early days, just like what Gregory and a few other guys did, and it was time to start worrying how we could distinguish Bill from everybody else." Bill's first reaction to that problem was, of course, a joke: "Some people call me the Philadelphia Dick Gregory, but that's silly. I'm taller and better-looking." More seriously, he commented, "I found that to be a success I'd have to jump over Dick Gregory. I had the shadow of Gregory in everything I did."

Later, Bill was able to explain their differences clearly. "I love Dick," he told a reporter in 1967, "and we're good friends. But there's no compari-

son between us. Dick has always been a specifically Negro comedian in the sense that his material
comes from the fact that he's Negro. Mine doesn't.
I'm just a comedian who happens to be a Negro. I
don't have the guts to do what Dick does, either
on the floor or off it," Bill continued. "Dick's
very involved in the freedom movement, leading
marches, picketing, going to jail. Not me. There's
no way possible you could get me to sit at a lunch
counter and have some S.O.B. bust a catsup bottle
over my head without one of us getting killed—
probably me."

So, by late 1963, all the racial material had been
removed from Bill's act, and none of it was recorded. His real interest was in remembering the
events of his childhood, both at home and on the
streets, and using them as comedy material. He
wanted to make those experiences appeal to everyone's memories of childhood. As he put it, "It
was everybody's neighborhood, always had been,
always will be."

Matt Robinson, an old friend of Bill Cosby's
who is also a writer (and now employed on *The
Cosby Show*), has recalled how Bill always spent
a lot of time soaking up stories about the kids in
the neighborhood. "Few people understand the
importance of Bill's background in his development as a storyteller and performer. For example,
he went to Temple and I went to Penn State, and
we both had summer jobs at municipal swimming
pools. I'd say, 'The kids at my pool take the soap
home.' Bill, with his wonderful sense of exaggera-

tion, would top me with, 'The kids at *my* pool bring their laundry.' Bill's sources of material come not only from his own family, but from all the families he grew up with in Philadelphia. Because there wasn't much formal entertainment, like movies or theater, in our neighborhoods, we entertained ourselves. On porches and in backyards, we told the funny things that happened to us at home. Bill sopped it all up like a sponge.''

At the beginning of his career, Bill Cosby was often underrated by critics who were misled by his casual, storytelling approach to comedy. Writing in *Hifi/Stereo Review,* the acronymic P. K. said, ''Mr. Cosby, actually only a moderately funny fellow, is an affable enough companion for an hour or so as he tells the listener about his journeys on New York subways ('They put a nut in every car'), mocks, not too successfully, the performances of ball players in razor blade commercials, tells about the hazards of attending a karate school, and delivers some curious insights into the character of Superman. A prolonged, rather fumbling routine about God's dialogue with Noah ends mercifully with the sound of rain. Cosby is a Negro performer who seems willing to leave politics to Dick Gregory, and his recording is an encounter with a pleasant, promising, but somewhat undisciplined talent.''

The same reviewer also criticized Bill's second album, *I Started Out As a Child.* He complained, ''I found his childhood memories—street football, corduroy pants, the art of wearing sneakers, and his father's terrifying way of snoring—funny at times, but too familiar." He concluded the review with his analysis of the problem: "Most comedians don't know when to stop, but Cosby's trouble, I believe, is that he doesn't know when to go on. Instead of developing his comic ideas, he abandons them almost as soon as they are born." That may have been the mark of an extremely creative young comedian; he had so many ideas that he was able to use some of them as throwaway material. Other comics would have developed these ideas into twenty-minute monologues. The critic for the *American Record Guide* also felt that Bill's comedic ideas needed more development. "Cosby's style is genial and very soothing. He starts out as a child, reminiscing about the old neighborhood where the kids played street football and a new pair of sneakers was a luxury not lightly come by; where he and his brother were reduced to stealing coins from their father's trousers pockets on Saturday nights and fretted about being cheated out of their own modest ration of Christmas gifts by an irascible Santa Claus. . . . All quite cozy and wistful. But is it humor? Only occasionally. More often Cosby's monologues, despite an assortment of grunts, wheezes, and sound effects, slide into a schmaltz-lubricated niche. . . ."

When you listen to the albums today (and it certainly says something about the timeless quality of Bill Cosby's humor that both of these twenty-year-old albums are still in print), you are struck primarily by the comedian's youthfulness. His voice

Chapter Five

I Spy Fame on Its Way

BILL COSBY'S APPEARANCE on *The Tonight Show* when Allan Sherman was a guest host was to have far-reaching repercussions.

He did his "karate school" routine, which starts out mildly poking fun at the number of people taking karate lessons ("twenty-three million schools in Greenwich Village alone"). It gets funnier and funnier as he imagines the disastrous results of overconfidence on the part of a karate school graduate who begins to look for dark alleys where he can stroll with ten-dollar bills hanging all over him. There are some of the inimitable Cosby sound effects, including swishing blows and the karate shout, and the usual, rather mocking punch line: When the karate expert whirls to demolish his attacker, he misses completely because the mugger is a midget.

One man watching the show that night was producer Sheldon Leonard. His credits on TV included *The Danny Thomas Show*, *The Dick Van Dyke Show*, and *The Andy Griffith Show*—a solid string of long-running hits. He was at that time mulling over an idea for a new series. "I wanted to do an adventure with comedy," Leonard explained. "I wanted the show to be about a couple of fellows whose relationship was deep and friendly. I had a script that would more or less do for the concept I was striving for, but I had no cast in mind other than a list of maybe a dozen solid, professional guys who might play either part." Finally, he selected Robert Culp for one role: Culp was an experienced off-Broadway actor and the veteran of several westerns on the tube. All Leonard had to do was find the other guy—someone whose chemistry would click with Culp's and give the show the warmth and extra dimension of humanity he was looking for.

Then he saw Bill Cosby on television, and shortly thereafter went to watch him work live at a club. Leonard recalls that he said to himself, " 'Geez, he would be perfect, if only . . .' And then I stopped right there, because I realized 'if only' was a condition I was creating myself." Still, aware that many other people might create the same condition, Leonard moved somewhat cautiously. "I make an intensive underground investigation before choosing a person for a long-range project of this sort. From every source I learned Bill Cosby was a tireless worker, a man striving to do his best. I called Grant Tinker of NBC and told him I had found a young comedian who had every quality we were looking for. 'In one way he is different,' I said. 'He is colored.' 'That's just great,' Tinker said. 'I think I speak for everyone at NBC when I say that.' ''

So Bill was given a screen test, and it turned out as Sheldon Leonard expected. Bill was able to project warmth as well as humor, and he had the athletic look that was right for the part of the tennis pro turned spy. Bill got the job.

From the beginning everyone insisted that Bill's color was not a consideration, and that the part would not be written to exploit the fact that he was black and costar Culp was white. Grant Tinker said, ''We did not set out to get a Negro to star in a feature. We think it is right and proper, but it was not planned in any sense.'' Bob Culp said dryly, ''An absence of a statement was the idea.'' Bill Cosby later commented, ''A lot of people were thoroughly messed up about the show in the beginning. They saw a black man and they thought NBC was trying to prove that Negroes were good actors or something. I just think Sheldon Leonard was looking for a human being, he saw Bill Cosby and liked him.''

Bill Cosby played the part of Alexander Scott, a CIA agent who also happens to be an excellent tennis player, a Rhodes scholar, and a master of seven languages. Camouflaging himself as a trainer/companion, he accompanies another spy, Kelly Robinson, played by Robert Culp, who is disguised as an international tennis bum, on secret missions all over the world. Along the way, they best the bad guys, meet the good girls, get tangled up with the bad girls, but always end up back in the fold of the good guys.

The series, called *I Spy,* was expensively produced. Each episode cost about $200,000 to create, which was at least $50,000 more than any comparable action adventure. Many of the episodes were filmed on location all over the world. Accustomed as we've now become to police stories that take place almost entirely in the squad room and detective stories that take place in someone's office, *I Spy* seems surprisingly rich and varied in its locations, and authentic in its details.

Bill Cosby was the first to admit that the change from comedy to acting was a tough one for him. His first reaction when he was offered the job was, "I wasn't afraid of the racial thing, but the acting. It was a personal quest: Can I do the job? Can this comedian turn into an actor?" Once he started rehearsals, he told an interviewer, "As a comedian, I was in command, directing myself and writing my own material. As an actor, what I am doing should be right on the button, but I am still tumbling around the fringes of performances—playing with the outside edge. I've been trying to do the story lines without camping—to get a laugh as an actor, not as a comedian, and it's not easy.'' Sheldon Leonard agreed. ''At first, he mumbled everything. He didn't listen to other people's lines, so he didn't react properly.''

Bill was blessed by the help of his more experienced costar, Robert Culp. The two men became friends right away, and Culp always stressed the similarities rather than the differences between them. ''Bill and I are on exactly the same wavelength. We're both bright, we're both shy, we're both competitive, and we seem to have gone through life with the same attitudes and outlook—don't fight it, baby, wait your time and psych it through. Whatever you say about one of us is almost sure to be true of the other one, too. I'll give you an example. I grew up in middle-class California, which had to be light-years from Bill's Philadelphia, but my childhood was such that I knew damn well I would have been in the nuthouse if it weren't for athletics. Guess what my specialty was? Also track, the loner's sport.''

Bill in his turn freely acknowledges his debt to Bob Culp. ''When we started, I didn't even know how to walk so that it looked right. I don't think we shot a scene for months when Bob didn't have to tell me what to do and how to do it. 'Hold the gun this way. . . . Face the camera when you bend down. . . . React to this line. . . .' There was just no end to it. What it amounted to is Bob was doing two full-time jobs—playing his part and coaching me in mine. I'd be nowhere if it weren't for him.''

Quite recently Bill revealed just how true that statement really was. He told a reporter in the spring of 1985, "When I was hired to do *I Spy*, I was so bad in my first segment that I was an embarrassment even to myself. And the word came down from one of the executives: 'Get rid of Cosby.' '' Bob Culp then picked up the story. "Bill was a rank beginner at acting. After the network executives viewed our pilot, I got this phone call from Sheldon Leonard, and he said, 'They want to fire Bill.' I said, 'Fine, let them fire him—but they'll have to fire me, too.' Sheldon said, 'Don't fly off the handle. They're only talking about firing Bill.' I said, 'Look, you can't learn to act overnight. Just give me a little time to work with Bill.' '' The executives did . . . and the rest, as they say, is history.

Most insiders agree that one reason for the big success of *I Spy* was that the friendship of the two stars spilled over into the on-screen drama, making it at once more believable and more involving to audiences. A technician on the show remembers how the two stars worked together. "Once we were doing a sequence where they had to scale a sheer twenty-foot wall of a building, run along a pitched roof, and jump a seven- or eight-foot alley to get to another roof. The idea was that you would see them start out, then we'd pull back for long shots, and stuntmen would actually do the climbing and the running. Them two? Before we had the scene, they were having conferences for an hour, shushing and shushing and breaking themselves up. Finally we started shooting. We get the close shots, and then these nuts go right on ahead, scaling the wall, running the roof, jumping the alley—having a ball. The camera wasn't rolling and they knew it, but everybody on the set was having a fit. There they were, laughing like a couple of kids stealing cookies.''

Actor Bob Culp has the last word on the subject. "I think audiences care less about a crackerjack script than the people they see on the screen. It's the chemistry of those people playing together that builds a following, and I guess it's pretty obvious on screen as well as off that Bill and I have a great regard for each other."

The success of *I Spy* was immediate and overwhelming. In its first season, the show began to appear regularly in the top twenty ratings. Despite some residual fears by NBC's executives about whether or not the casting of a black star would make some Southern stations refuse to take the show, all but four of the two hundred affiliates carried it. Even the reviews were good. Bill was especially gratified by one that appeared in *The New York Times* in September 1965, after the first episode was aired: "Mr. Cosby effortlessly demonstrated that he could develop into a promising actor." No one knew better than Bill how wrong the adverb "effortlessly" was, but the fact that it looked that way indicated that he had succeeded in giving the kind of relaxed performance he had been aiming for.

In the spring of 1966, when the nominees for television's Emmy Awards were announced, both Bill and Bob had been nominated for Best Actor in a Dramatic Series. On top of that, Bill had been asked to cohost the ceremonies. He looked very elegant in his white tie and tails . . . and he looked very surprised when it was announced that he had won the Emmy for Best Actor. It was an emotion-filled moment for Bill. Of course, he was thrilled by the honor. But at the same time he was sad that his win meant his friend Bob Culp had lost. In his acceptance speech, he said bluntly, "Bob lost this because he helped me." It may have been this experience that initiated Bill's distaste for competing with his peers. Culp, ever the gentleman, refused to discuss the subject of his own disappointment and simply said he was looking forward to starting a second season of the show.

Ratings and awards notwithstanding, there were still critics of *I Spy,* and especially of the role of Alexander Scott. Some people pointed out that in order for a black man to be considered the equal of a white tennis bum, he had to be an Ivy League graduate, a Rhodes scholar, and impossibly accomplished in a number of fields. The same people complained that Alexander Scott's role of trainer implicitly made him Kelly's subordinate, not far removed from the traditional black man's role of valet.

Perhaps most significant was the way the shows generally ended. Kelly Robinson was usually shown in the arms of a ravishing beauty, like James Bond in the books and movies. But Scotty was back in his room reading a book or falling asleep, some thought suspiciously like a eunuch. Bill himself complained about this aspect of the series, saying, "If Alexander Scott doesn't get to go out with a girl once in a while, people are going to wonder about me." Producer Sheldon Leonard explained one reason for his reluctance to let Scotty get the girl. "I am not going to feed the concept that says a Negro only responds to the sex drive. We want him to have girls, but there has to be sweetness and dignity to it."

On one point, Bill Cosby was adamant. On the occasions when he did get the girl, she would be of his own race. One of the women he did play a love scene with was the glamorous and beautiful Eartha Kitt. She later gave him high praise for his talent, saying, "It usually takes an artist at least fifteen years to become as relaxed as he is naturally. He's fine to work with." Bill later explained his stand on this racial sexual issue. "It was my decision right from the start to play it that way. As long as I'm on the screen, whether television or films, I will never hold or kiss a white woman. Our black women have just nothing to look forward to in films, nothing to identify with. Sure, you see the black man trying to get the white woman, maybe, and failing. Or you see the black woman being installed by the ranch owner or fore-man . . . for what? To make love to a white man, never a black man. Tell me, how often do you see a black man falling in love and making love with a black woman? So, as it is, I want to be seen only with our women. . . .''

Bill's remarks indicate that, no matter how much he publicly downplayed the issue of race, he was aware that he was breaking new ground for other black performers. The point was hammered at by nearly every critic and journalist who discussed the series. For example, one reporter said, even before the first show had aired, ''A lot rides on how well Cosby does. If the series does succeed, money in Hollywood will suppose it is because a Negro is in an unroutine role. If it doesn't, failure will be supposed for the same reason.'' Sheldon Leonard summed it up: ''He's got a hell of a dilemma. He's in danger of rejection because he isn't shar-ing their struggle, their pain, or their militancy.''

When Bill did discuss this aspect of his star-dom, he chose his words very carefully: ''The show is exhilarating in some ways and a burden in others. The character I play is a highly educated man, and I'm nowhere near that. I was never a great student, although in my freshman year I was so frightened that I made myself do well. And he is a Negro 'good guy' working equally with a white man for a patriotic cause—a premise which may not be accepted by every Negro watching. In other words, though the part is never the usual put-down of the Negro people, I feel I have to be careful that it doesn't become an exaggeration of another kind. I hope we don't feel any artificial praise—for the wrong reasons. I'd like *I Spy* to be judged on its entertainment values." Several years later, Bill spoke more directly about the situation when he said, "Sheldon Leonard was my Branch Rickey [the baseball manager who made Jackie Robinson the first black to play in the major leagues]. Everybody's always comparing me with Jackie Robinson . . . but the thing of it is, you don't want to look at the first Negro doing a thing and say, 'Wow, boy!' It's the man who had the guts to give the break who really counts."

In the end, Bill felt he had achieved his goal. "Audiences see two guys, not Bob Culp, white, and Bill Cosby, Negro." Bob Culp pointed out what an achievement that matter-of-fact acceptance really was. "We're two guys who don't know the difference between a colored and a white man. That's doing more than a thousand marches. We're showing what it could be like if there had been no hate."

Ratings of *I Spy* continued to be high during its second season, and once again, Bill Cosby won an Emmy for Best Actor in a Dramatic Series. He repeated his triumph in the 1968–69 season, making it three Emmys in a row. But the show began to decline in the ratings, perhaps rendered obsolete by the real live war in Vietnam that viewers watched on their screens every night. CIA agents were no longer universally regarded as "good guys," and the blend of comedy and adventure rang a bit hollow at a time of such national discord about whether or not the sacrifice of lives was really necessary. In the spring of 1969, Sheldon Leonard decided that the time for *I Spy* was over.

The value to Bill Cosby of his early success in a television series watched by thirty million viewers was simply incalculable. He had gone from being a rising young comedian to being a nationally recognized star. Bill knew he had traveled a long distance from the streets of Philadelphia. He tried to explain the difference to interviewer Joanne Stang: "As an *I Spy* star, I'm a part of the NBC team, and as such I'm—not deferred to, really, but respected and protected. This is difficult to express, but that's an odd feeling for the average Negro." He concluded thoughtfully, "Financially, I'm a big success, I guess. But I realize that the money doesn't really matter. It's the dignity I'm working for."

No doubt Bill was sincere when he made that comment, but of course the money helped him acquire things he never thought he'd have. By the last season of *I Spy*, he was earning $750,000 for his participation. Moreover, his increased fame had enabled him to charge $25,000 a week when he appeared at Harrah's in Tahoe during the summer. And when the show went on the air in the fall of 1965, the sale of his comedy albums immediately tripled. The role of Alexander Scott gave Bill Cosby financial security of the sort he'd never dreamed he would be able to achieve. At last he could give his mother all the things he'd always wanted her to have, and he could give his younger brothers the help that would allow them to create their own secure futures.

And Bill had one other reason to be glad that he no longer had to worry about money. Now he had a family of his own.

Chapter Six

The "Wonderfulness" of a Family

I thought kids were the simplest little creatures in the world, once upon a time. That was before I had any of my own. But me, I'm someone who likes to do things in the overkill method. I had a kid—my wife helped, of course—and then another and another and . . . well, you get the picture.

EVEN IF YOU HAD NEVER heard a word about Bill Cosby's personal life, you probably wouldn't be very surprised to hear that he is happily married and loves his family. He is simply too nice for fans to imagine him any other way.

It all began back in 1963, when Bill was playing The Shadows, a club in Washington. According to the story told by writer Joel Cohen, a friend arranged a blind date for him while he was in town. He was to meet the girl in a bowling alley. Being Bill Cosby, the first thing he did was tease the girl about the weakness of her game.

Her name was Camille Hanks, and she was a nineteen-year-old student at the University of Maryland, majoring in psychology. Her father was a research chemist at Walter Reed Hospital, and her mother directed a nursery school. She was a well-brought-up young lady, who also happened to be bright and beautiful. Bill said, "The first time I saw her, I said, 'I'm going to marry her.' I just liked her." Bill Cosby, of course, can't resist a little joke about the situation. "She was corny, straight ahead, you know. I said, 'I'll take her and mold her.' "

For her part, Camille enjoyed Bill's company. He made her laugh—even about her own low score in bowling. And when she went to The Shadows a few days later to watch him perform, she realized that he was a very talented comedian. Luckily for Bill, Camille realized that he could be a big success in his entertainment career. Her parents, however, didn't quite look at it the same way. To them, Bill Cosby was a college dropout who had chosen a very precarious way of making a living. They had grave doubts about his suitability for their daughter. Bill clearly remembers his future mother-in-law's attitude. "On that first visit, I was making $450 a week, and when I went back, I was making $750. Her mother was suspicious about that. She didn't see how I could be making so much money. Anyway, she didn't want any entertainer running away with her daughter."

Bill understood the reason for her parents' objections to him, but he persisted. He carried on a long-distance courtship that was nothing short of exhausting. When his stint at The Shadows was over, he was booked back at The Bitter End in New York. He worked until three or four in the morning, making it virtually impossible to see Camille. But love found a way. Bill would sleep until nine A.M., get up, and drive the two hundred miles to Maryland in time to take Camille out to lunch and maybe a movie in the afternoon. Then he hopped back into his rattletrap car and hurried back another two hundred miles to New York, arriving in time to shower and change before he had to get over to the club to start work.

Mr. and Mrs. Hanks, who had perhaps hoped that the romance would cool off when Bill was no longer working in Washington, took a dim view of the situation. Finally, they decided to send Camille away to stay with relatives in Virginia for a while, hoping she would forget Bill. This strategy did cool things down temporarily, but in the end, love triumphed. Camille and Bill decided to get married, and her parents reluctantly agreed. The wedding took place on January 25, 1964, in Olney, Maryland, just a few miles from Camille's home.

Their honeymoon must have been enough to confirm the Hanks's worst fears about the life their daughter would lead married to Bill. He was booked to appear in New York, at the now defunct club called Basin Street East, on their wedding night. So he spent most of the night on stage. It's not exactly the way a girl dreams of spending her wedding night, and the rest of the honeymoon went pretty much the same way. Bill's bookings had to take first place in their lives, and their free time was built around his schedule.

It must have been a difficult adjustment for

Camille. She was then, and still remains, a very private person. She's not the type who enjoys hanging out at a club all night, nor does she want to live her life in the public eye. Bill, too, guards his privacy, but he understood from the beginning that a certain amount of publicity was a requirement in his chosen line of work. As he explained several years after their marriage, "She hates photographers around the house. But once in a while I have to have them. I could get by without it, but I think it's important to have pictures of a Negro family with Momma and Poppa around, living in decent surroundings." So, gradually, the couple began to work out a life-style with which they could both feel comfortable.

Camille's preference for a settled family life must have seemed to her unattainable in that first year of marriage, as Bill appeared all over the United States and Canada, playing clubs for a week or two at a time and then moving on. The young couple moved into the Cosby house in Philadelphia, but Bill was away most of the time. When he got the role in *I Spy* in 1965, it proved to be as beneficial to his personal life as it was to his career. It gave Bill and Camille a home base, in Los Angeles, and after a while, it also provided the money to buy a comfortable house. The one they eventually chose must have seemed palatial from the perspective of a boy who grew up on the Philadelphia streets; but, in fact, for a big television star, it was relatively modest. It was about twenty-five years old, built in the Spanish style with a red tile roof (that leaked when it rained), and decorated by Camille in a tasteful and understated way. Of course, you have to remember that it *was* Hollywood, so the house had a swimming pool, a sauna, and a billiards room. It also had a bedroom for a permanently honored guest, Bill's mother, Mrs. Anna Cosby.

And it had room for plenty of children. When Bill signed to do *I Spy*, Camille was expecting their first child. Bill was apparently so convinced it was going to be a boy that he had an ad prepared to run in *Variety* as soon as the child was born, reading, "I got the first man for my softball team." Bill was in Hong Kong shooting the *I Spy* pilot when he got the word that a baby had been born on April 8, 1965, a girl. Bill ran the ad anyway, adding at the bottom a big "Oops!" followed by the words, "We'll treat her as if she was our son."

According to a rare interview with Camille Cosby, Bill threw himself into the responsibilities of fatherhood. "As a father, he's a very gentle man. He's just crazy about the baby and so patient. He loves to bathe her and feed her and dress her. He's just a very loving father. As a husband, he has the same qualities." But even when it comes to life's most tender moments, Bill never loses his sense of humor. When someone asked him, shortly before the birth, what they were going to call the new baby, he answered, "Haven't decided on the baby's name yet. Just gonna send him out to play, and whatever the kids call him, that's his name." In fact, Camille was the one who chose the name of Erika Ranee.

For the rest of that year, Camille and the baby traveled with Bill when he went on location with *I Spy*, and it was obvious that they enjoyed the chance to be together. But Camille's travels came to a halt early in 1966, when she was once again pregnant. Bill was certain that it would be a boy this time—and he was also determined that this time he was going to be around to share in the exciting moments. He had carefully arranged his schedule to have free time in mid-August when the baby was expected. But, as often happens, the baby ignored the carefully planned schedule. Camille went into labor several weeks early, as Bill was about to leave the house to fly to Denver for an appearance. He stayed with her until the birth of their second child—another girl—and then chartered a Lear jet to arrive in Denver ten minutes before showtime. The new baby was named Erinn Chalene.

Although Bill humorously complained about the fact that his baby daughters couldn't play basketball, he loved to spend time with them. The family swam together in the pool and played the imaginary games Bill remembered from his own childhood. And Camille and the girls continued to travel with Bill whenever it was feasible.

In 1969, the Cosbys had their third child and first son. Bill named him Ennis. When a reporter asked about the origin of the name, Bill said he made it up, and that it meant ''trust nobody, and smile." Four years later, in 1973, another daughter, Ensa, was born. The Cosbys' fifth child, daughter Evin, came along in 1976. Bill had his basketball team . . . but only if he dropped his snobbishness and let the girls play, too.

As Hollywood couples go, the Cosbys make extremely boring reading. What's a gossip columnist to do with a star who seems genuinely devoted to his wife and goes around saying nice things about her? Typical quotes: "I wish Camille on every husband. That's the only way I can describe her. She's as feminine as any woman can be. She has great taste. And without realizing it, she has a sense of humor. This is Camille: I said, 'Come into this new sauna bath.' So she came in and I asked her what she thought of it. Her answer was, 'It's hot in here,' and she split, man!" Or, "I am happiest when Camille is happy. And that's often. She's not a goer, doesn't like all the phony show-biz things. I understand that." Or, "My wife works very, very hard at being probably one of the greatest mothers." See what I mean? There's nothing here that could start even the tiniest of rumors.

When someone asked Bill Cosby how he liked to spend his spare time, he cracked, "I just drive home from the studio and stare at the wife and kids." It's one of those jokes that isn't far from the truth. His life, since his marriage, has been basically home-centered. Despite the big house, and the Mercedes and the Lincoln Continental in the driveway, Bill Cosby's life still has a lot in common with his childhood in Philadelphia. Family comes first, then close friends. In the period between 1965 and 1971, when the Cosbys lived full-time in Hollywood, their house was a sort of headquarters for friends. They included Bob Culp and his wife, actress France Nuyen; jazz drummer Elvin Jones; boxer Muhammed Ali and basketball star Wilt Chamberlain; musicians Miles Davis and Harry Belafonte; actors Sidney Poitier, Henry Silva, and Sammy Davis. Bill says he's happiest when he has people around, so the Cosbys entertain frequently.

And even though he had achieved stardom, Bill hadn't forgotten the friends he made back in Philadelphia. He told a reporter, "I'll fly a bunch of my old high school buddies out here every once in a while for a week. They'll stay at my place, and we'll drink and talk and play pool and have a good time. It's fun, and it usually goes good, but now and then one of the guys will act strange. Like I'm changed, I'm not the old Bill Cosby he knew down on the corner. I guess it's because I'm in the public eye. I don't feel it, but the guy does. One guy I'd known twenty-five years came out and called me 'Mister Cosby.' Believe that? I didn't say anything. I let him call me it. I tried to figure if there really was something different about me. After some time things loosened up, a little friendlier, and the guy finally called me Shorty, my nickname from the old days. I corrected him: 'Mister Cosby to you,' I said, and we had a big laugh out of that, and from then on, things went along fine."

Don't think success changed Bill Cosby's attitude toward his mother, either. He still shows her all the respect he did when he was a kid. One of the things that made him happiest about his newfound wealth was that it meant he could do all the things for her he had always wanted to. He offered her a house of her own in California, but she said she preferred to live in her own house in Philadelphia, where she would be in familiar surroundings. So Bill paid off the mortgage and fixed up the house to give her every comfort and convenience. Just for good measure, he threw in two fur coats and a brand-new car.

Bill Cosby's feet were firmly planted on the ground. Unlike most stars, he didn't have an entourage of ego-boosting hangers-on. He wanted to keep his kids down-to-earth, too. He was the kind of father who worried about their grades and wouldn't let them get away with acting "Hollywood." And he was careful to keep his own growing affluence from giving them unrealistic expectations.

Bill's one personal extravagance is cars. He's owned a number of different cars: a Rolls-Royce vintage model, a Rover, a maroon Ferrari. He even tried having a chauffeur, but he decided it was no fun sitting in the back of the car. He likes to drive himself, and during the years he lived in Hollywood, he had a cure for the mounting tensions of life in that glamorous fishbowl. He'd simply get in his car, head for a deserted highway in the middle of the night, and give the Ferrari its head. "It's kind of like getting away from everybody," he explained. But he went on to add, "I don't punish the car. I just get in the car and take my daughter or somebody, and we just go for a little spin. There's nobody around. It's just kind of a way to get away from it all."

The pressures of sudden stardom can get to even the sanest people. Along with the success and the money come the problems: the loss of privacy, the intricacies of contract terms and financial management, the important career decisions that shape the future, and perhaps most devastating, the fear of failure. Bill Cosby coped with these problems better than most people, but he, too, was faced with tough decisions about his future. Once *I Spy* was over, what should he do next? How could he follow up that kind of success?

Chapter Seven

The Big Star on the Little Screen

In show business, you can be rich today and back in the projects tomorrow.

ACCORDING TO ONE INFORMED report, Bill Cosby had earned over $2 million by the time *I Spy* went off the air. The estimate seems, if anything, a bit conservative. With the salary Bill made for the TV show, the royalties he received from his fast-selling comedy albums, and the rising fees for his personal appearances, he was certainly doing well. And Bill was not the man to let that kind of money run through his fingers. Instead, he did what many other stars have done in the same situation. He used the money he had made to finance his own new ventures, thereby enabling him both to maintain creative control and to get the lion's share of future profits generated by his own talents.

With manager Roy Silver and another business

partner, producer Bruce Campbell, he formed Campbell Silver Cosby Corporation. The company had handsome offices on Canon Drive, in Beverly Hills, just a few convenient miles away from Bill Cosby's home. Campbell Silver Cosby itself owned a number of production companies, including Jemmin Productions to make television shows and Tetragrammaton to produce and distribute records. There was also a corporate arm that handled public relations and one that was responsible for personal management. Needless to say, the central asset of all these businesses was Bill Cosby, who was also the chief shareholder and executive vice-president of the company. Although certain aspects of this business arrangement made Bill uneasy from the start, he did appreciate the opportunity to manage his own career and make his own choices about future projects.

Another television series seemed not just natural but inevitable. Television was where Bill Cosby had won his first big fame, and where he would continue to have his greatest successes. In fact, he had the perfect television personality: warm, relaxed, and kind—just the sort of person viewers would like to invite into their living rooms every week.

So it was with high hopes that Bill embarked on his second series. He was to be his own executive producer, and to a great extent, he was responsible for the initial concept of the show. Called *The Bill Cosby Show*, it starred Bill as Chet Kincaid, a physical education teacher—perhaps the very man

Bill Cosby once thought he would grow up to be. At the outset, he was very enthusiastic about both the character and the series concept. He described Chet Kincaid as "a human being who is a school-teacher. In other words, he makes mistakes, gets into trouble, and reflects quite frequently on the human condition. . . . The character I play will do certain things that will provoke anger. What I'm really doing is a study of human behavior. My actions will be deplorable sometimes, but by being that way, I'm saying to the audience, 'Are you really that pure? . . . What are you like when nobody's looking?' That's the person I'm interested in. My character will do all those things a person does when eyes aren't on him. He'll put his feet up on the desk, jump on the trampoline with his shoes on, and frequently act out of selfish motives. . . . They'll look at him and see something they don't like, and then ask themselves if they do the same thing or are like that. I'll make Chet Kincaid do anything I want him to do. I will make him physically and verbally say what's really in his mind."

In other words, Chet Kincaid was sort of an alter ego for Bill Cosby, as well as a vehicle for a message or two about human nature. Moreover, Bill was determined that the show would demonstrate the benefits of a good education, and he even invited educators to look at some of the episodes before they were aired, checking the classroom scenes to make sure they showed examples of good teaching.

The Bill Cosby Show seems to have been so burdened with good intentions that it was handicapped from the very beginning. The complex character Bill intended Chet Kincaid to be was so difficult to pull off that most viewers simply never understood who he was. Bill had told a reporter, "There are times when Chet will miss the point. He may be looking for something and it may be right in front of his nose. I do this deliberately, figuring that people will identify with Chet and become better teachers, better mothers, better fathers."

The first episode of the series was aired in September of 1969, just one year after *I Spy* went off the air. A reviewer for *Variety* complained, "Cosby played the role unconvincingly, and his tendency to exaggerate the character's light-heartedness diminished the whimsy of the situations." Nevertheless, *The Bill Cosby Show* was the top-rated new show of the season. The sheer likability of Bill Cosby triumphed over the problems of his material.

Yet there continued to be criticism of the material. One essay attacking the show appeared in *The New York Times* in December of 1969. It was written by Faith Berry, a black critic, and the main indictment she leveled was that the show did nothing for the black man's image, since there was nothing about Chet Kincaid that was in any way black, except that he happened to be played by a black actor. She dismissed the show as "irrelevant."

Bill himself continued to believe that he could

best serve the interests of black people by simply showing them to be human. He refused to be identified as a "problem" but insisted on being seen as part of the human race. It was his feeling that, in the long run, this was the best way he could combat racial stereotypes. In his opinion, if viewers didn't think of Chet Kincaid as specifically black, then he was doing his job right.

Unfortunately, the ratings slipped by the end of the first season, and although the show was renewed for a second season, the ratings got worse and worse. It was no surprise to anyone when the show was canceled in the spring of 1971.

Meanwhile, Bill continued to appear on TV in his specials. *The First Bill Cosby Special* aired in the spring of 1968, while *I Spy* was still running, and it was a big success in the ratings. That led inevitably to *The Second Bill Cosby Special* in 1969 and *The Third Bill Cosby Special* in 1970. All three specials focused primarily on Bill's own comedy and gave him lots of time to do his funny monologues. The second special, for example, contained the long Noah sketch. It was augmented but not changed by the presence of a troupe of dancers, and it set the audience up for a long story about the way Bill used to fight with his brother Russell, and another long story about going to church with Fat Albert. The most important guest of the evening was Mrs. Anna Cosby, introduced from the audience. In the third special, the guest was Roberta Flack. These specials were widely praised by critics, who noted their superior production values, their tight focus on what the star did best, their restrained use of dancers and elaborate costumes.

The specials were produced by Bill Cosby's company, Campbell Silver Cosby (CSC). But in the late 1960s, CSC was undergoing explosive change. Bill had publicly expressed his reservations about the way the company was being run. In an interview with *Life* journalist Thomas B. Morgan, in the spring of 1969, Bill said candidly, "I used to let Silver make more of the decisions. Now I make most of them. This corporation is his idea. His biggest dream—way overextended. . . . I guess I have some business talent. But I also feel as creative as ever. I can be a businessman and a straight actor and a comic and do it all well."

Bill had entered into the business arrangement of the corporation primarily because he wanted the chance to have creative control of his enterprises. It was the business end of things that had begun to worry him, and a lot of the problem was a difference in philosophy between himself and Roy Silver. Silver, obviously well attuned to the "go-go" concept popular on Wall Street in the 1960s, thought the company should be what financiers call "highly leveraged." In plain English that means working with a lot of other people's borrowed money. The good part about it is that a lot more can be done with this borrowed money than with limited personal funds. The bad part, of course, is that the company is immediately plunged deeply into debt.

Bill favored a much more conservative approach.

He explained it several years later in this way: "Say you owe $800,000 in taxes. An adviser tells you that to protect your earnings it's best to buy yourself a $10 million shopping complex. Now, my wife and I come from the kind of neighborhood where you feel good when you pay your bills. Like you pay for your house and feel good when it's all paid for. This other way—first, all you owe is $800,000. Then you make an investment, and you're $10 million in debt. It doesn't make sense. We don't want to be overinvested. We want to pay for things."

Unfortunately, Roy Silver's way of running the company made Bill Cosby feel continually overinvested. Whatever the merits of such an approach might be in financial terms, Bill found that he was personally uncomfortable, As he said to Roy while journalist Morgan was present, "Roy, your concept and my concept of how to run a business are different." The result of this difference was that the partners split. According to one estimate, Campbell Silver Cosby Productions had at that time contracts worth nearly $30 million. But regardless of how much he stood to make, Bill wanted out.

Corporate partnerships are almost as difficult to end as marriages, and the "divorce" can be just as bitter. Gentleman that he is, Bill tried to maintain a dignified silence about the situation, even in the face of pointed and very personal questions from interviewers. But the breakup of the corporation left Bill in an awkward situation professionally. The majority of those signed contracts controlled by CSC were for his own services. Even though he had left CSC, he still had to honor those contracts for CSC-controlled projects; if he didn't, he would be blamed by others for not living up to his contractual obligations.

It says a lot for Bill's professionalism that he not only lived up to those obligations but did his work well, in spite of the circumstances. For example, his second TV special was being made for the network by CSC's Jemmin Productions, and Roy Silver was the executive producer. It couldn't have been easy for the two men to work together every day, but Bill never let the personal situation interfere with his performance. Luckily, the terms of his contract gave him creative control, so at least in that important area he was his own master.

Another project dear to Bill Cosby's heart was launched at about the same time, also under the auspices of CSC (until the contract problems could be worked out and the rights could be held by Bill alone). That was the first animated appearance of *Fat Albert and The Cosby Kids*. The characters were drawn from Bill's stand-up comedy routines about his childhood in Philadelphia. They were comic versions of real people he had known on the streets and in school—and, as Bill liked to point out, they were characters that *everybody* knew in their own childhood. There was Fat Albert, oversized and inclined to act like a bully whenever he thought he could get away with it. There was Old Weird Harold, tall and thin and frequently spaced out. Dumb Donald was the perennial fall guy, and

Rudy the Rich was the one who liked to boast about what he had that the other kids in the gang didn't.

All of these characters were well known to Cosby fans, and the special spread their fame. The kids themselves were animated cartoons; Bill provided their voices and also appeared in person for a bit of lead-in narration. The special was such a success when it aired in the fall of 1971 that network executives immediately began to think about how to make Fat Albert and the gang a part of their regular programming. This didn't happen until 1972, when CBS introduced a new Saturday morning show, *Fat Albert and The Cosby Kids*, at 12:30 P.M. Each show was introduced by Bill himself, and then he appeared again at the end to reinforce the message of the episode.

And there *was* a message. *Fat Albert* was conceived to be much more than mindless entertainment to keep the kids quiet while Mommy and Daddy slept late. Bill had a serious educational purpose: he wanted the show to teach kids proper behavior and values. To make sure that it happened, and that it was done right, he enlisted a distinguished panel of educators to act as advisers to the programs. The panel was headed by Gordon L. Berry, an assistant dean at UCLA, and Berry made it clear that he was going to take his responsibilities seriously. As he explained to columnist Kay Gardella, "When I selected the panel of advisers, I contacted prestigious people in the field of anthropology, psychiatry, sociology, child development, communication theory, and so forth. All of the team assembled are very busy. If they weren't giving their time for consultation on this project, they'd be doing several other things. So I naturally made it very clear that we would not merely provide a rubber stamp of approval for the network. Cosby, the writers, and other people connected with the network were pleased. So what we've been doing is going over the scripts and endings, concepts and ideas that involve proper child development. For instance, a script about a prankster was called to our attention. We agreed a program should be done about a prankster, but they should not show the kind of prank that traumatized a child or one that was hostile, such as the flower that squirts water. And in the case of the kid that's the prankster, there should be negative feedback.''

The amount of care that went into the writing of the show, and its pedagogical content, paid off. *Fat Albert and The Cosby Kids* was a program with high ratings that also won a number of awards. The audience was measured at about six million kids, all of whom just loved Bill Cosby. As he explained, ''I can be silly. I can be grown-up. I can be an older brother. I can be just a funny man that they know.'' The program won the Children's Theater Association Seal of Excellence in 1973 and a variety of educational awards for its positive influence on feelings, behavior, and value judgments. It's an achievement Bill Cosby can still be proud of.

Just before the *Fat Albert* series went on the air, Bill Cosby did two other special programs for children. One was a Saturday morning special called *A Day with Bill Cosby* that focused primarily on an antidrug message. The program started with Bill talking about his life and work, taking the viewers on a tour of the NBC studios, doing a little bit of his favorite Fat Albert routines. But the heart of the hour-long special was a discussion in a classroom setting by three experts on the drug problem. This was one of the first programs to recognize that drugs were not a problem confined to minority kids or urban ghettos but, in fact, affected children of all ages and all socioeconomic conditions. The experts were three men with the best of credentials: a textbook author, a priest who ran a halfway house for addicts, and a Harlem policeman. The producer/director explained that the intention of the program was to help the child viewer "to come to his own rational decision not to abuse drugs long before he is presented with an opportunity to do so. We want to build an attitude." Reviews praised the program for succeeding in what it set out to do.

In November of 1971, another Bill Cosby special aimed at children was broadcast. It was a dramatization of a selection of Aesop's fables, with Bill playing Aesop to a live audience of spellbound children; the fables themselves were done in animation with a lot of colorful effects. A review in *Christian Science Monitor* summed up the production's foremost message: "On CBS-

TV last night, *Aesop's Fables* probably confirmed for many people what they had been thinking all along about Bill Cosby: He can pull off nearly anything on television.''

But could he pull off another prime-time series? CBS was betting the answer was yes. Execs there believed that his tremendous personal popularity could carry another series, and after a period of negotiation, Bill agreed. The new show was to have a variety format, but—as was frequently the case with projects Bill undertook—it had some serious intentions underlying the fun. ''What we'll be doing is digging away at us humans and our foibles,'' explained Bill. ''What I want to do is establish myself as a storyteller. In our sketches, we're after feeling as well as comedy. We'll aim our observations at psychological hang-ups people might have. We'll be asking the audience, 'Are you that person?' We're trying to get underneath things, get inside, not just do the obvious.''

The show, called *The New Bill Cosby Show,* to distinguish it from its immediate predecessor, had the benefit of a lot of talent. First and foremost, of course, there was Bill Cosby. There was also the producer, George Schlatter, one of the creators of *Rowan and Martin's Laugh-In*. The musical director was none other than Quincy Jones. Regulars included the luscious Lola Falana, Susan Tolsky playing a ''dizzy dame'' character who never quite gets anything right, and Foster Brooks, as the inimitable drunken executive, setting the style for drunk acts of generations to come.

Schlatter tells a funny story about his first clash with his strong-willed star. "The first argument we had involved the set designer. Bill wanted the man who did *The Electric Company* sets. He insisted. I wanted the man who did *Ed Sullivan* for ten years." Schlatter smiles. "He turned out to be the same man, Bill Bohnert." But Schlatter was quite serious about what he saw as his mission: "The most important thing is to keep the show *Bill*."

The first show aired in September 1972, and had as guest stars Sidney Poitier and Harry Belafonte. As many reviewers noted, the chances of success for the show were slender because of the Monday night time slot that placed it up against high-rating Monday night football and NBC's blockbuster movie. The reviewer for *Variety* assessed the show this way: "Timing and pace are the major problems at the outset, a common curse of vidtape freedom, with overdrawn sketches and a tossed salad of elements slogging the midsection between lively production numbers. But it looks as though Cosby has the stand-up strength to helm an hour, especially with good guest support, which Sidney Poitier and Harry Belafonte for the most part supplied on the opener, and with the sort of oddball continuing characters former *Laugh-In* producer George Schlatter and director Mark Warren should be expert at casting and working."

The best part of the show was usually Bill's monologue, and the director always allowed the necessary time for Bill to build his stories just as he did in live appearances on stage. Despite a distinguished list of guests that included Buddy Hackett, Robert Culp, Roberta Flack, Don Rickles, Lily Tomlin, and Diahann Carroll, to name just a few, the rest of the show never held the interest that Bill alone on a stage could create. Ratings began to sink, and the show was canceled at the end of its first season.

For a while Bill was adamant about refusing to consider another series. He put his energies into other work and appeared on television only on occasional specials or as a guest on a talk show. But ABC execs were still convinced that Bill Cosby was destined for success in a weekly series, and they kept making offers until finally, in 1976, they made one he couldn't refuse. They gave him the chance to develop another variety series, but this time they gave him a time slot on Sunday night at seven P.M. and told him to do his best to create a show that the whole family would enjoy.

Bill liked the notion of a family show. He explained, "It has to do with something very, very technical. It has to do with using the tube to address itself to educational values, to teaching, to subjects that have to do with morals. What the networks are worried about is my show will be turned into a university instead of a variety hour, but my producer, Chris Beard, and I have guaranteed them that this hour will be funny without preaching and teaching." He went on to add, "I feel more comfortable in this Sunday spot—mainly because I feel that I know family and I know what family would like to see. I'd like to do more educational material, however, but in the end we're there to entertain.''

The show was called *Cos*, and the first episode of the series was broadcast in September 1976. An examination of the credits indicate that the list of writers was longer than the list of performers. The format of the show was to open and close with monologues from Bill, and to feature in the middle a one-on-one interview conducted by Bill with a child from the audience. The rest of the show leaned heavily on the variety format and included cameos by famous guest stars as well as short cartoon sequences.

In an interview given to Kay Gardella shortly before the series went on the air, Bill seemed somewhat defensive about this latest entry into series competition. He said, ''My first series, *I Spy*, ran three years. *The Bill Cosby Show* lasted two years. My first variety show lasted one year. And this show? If I'm lucky, it will run thirteen weeks.''

Cos was canceled after thirteen weeks. This time reviews were much less kind. *TV Guide*'s reviewer pronounced, ''*Cos* is the series that asks the musical question, 'Why is Bill Cosby so good and his show so bad?' The powers that be at ABC would probably like the answer to that one themselves. . . . *Cos* is the television equivalent of going down to the delicatessen to watch them run the bread slicer. The producers describe their series as entertainment 'the whole family can watch

together.' To that I say, bring back *Lassie*. At
least that show admitted that it was a dog. In
trying to be all things to all family members, *Cos*
winds up boring everybody. . . . It's really a shame,
because Cosby is one of the most talented and just
plain likable performers on TV today.'' The reviewer concluded that the show was just too cute
to live. As it turned out, he was right.

Bill accepted the cancellation philosophically.
He said, ''I have no animosity about TV, especially the fellows at ABC, because we did what we
felt the people would want to see. But it's a very
difficult area if you don't find the basic key. I
don't think I can handle a weekly variety show. It
has nothing to do with being too big for the me-
dium or with race or anything else. I just haven't
been able to put together the kind of show where
the public will say, 'Hey, let's watch!' It's as
simple as that.''

Nearly a decade would pass before Bill Cosby
would try another series . . . and finally achieve
the success he had been looking for. In the in-
terim, he had other aspects of his multifaceted
career to consider.

Chapter Eight

How to Be Funny Without Telling Jokes

> You're a talking cartoonist, painting images in the audience's head. If it sees the images as funny, then it laughs.

> When you go on stage, you're embarrassed to come right out and say, "Love me," but that's really what you're doing.

NO MATTER WHAT ELSE has occupied his time and attention, Bill Cosby has never stopped working on his comedy routines. Professionally, his comic monologues are the touchstone of his creativity and the foundation for all his other work. Even when he is working on a television series, he still tries to devote one day a week to writing his comedy material. And whenever his schedule permits, he appears before a live audience.

By the early seventies, Bill was able to command a fee of $40,000 to $50,000 a week for his one-man comedy show. He was always very careful about his selection of a venue, because he wanted to make sure his fans would be comfortable and able to enjoy themselves. He explained,

"I like to see my people comfortable, not crammed into a small club and paying a hefty cover charge. I have nothing against the night club business, but places like Madison Square Garden and the Westbury Music Fair are better. Westbury even more so, because the parking is better and people don't have to drive into the city. Plus they're not drinking and there's no extra tab laid on them." As the years went by he tended to restrict his appearances to certain clubs, such as Harrah's in Lake Tahoe, where he was accustomed to the surroundings and certain that both he and his fans would be well treated.

This sort of protectiveness was necessary as his fame grew along with his legions of fans. Club acts can be very draining. The late hours are hard, especially for performers with families and those who are used to the early morning starts demanded by working in films and TV. The performance itself is very demanding, since it requires staying "on" for several hours at a time, several shows a night. And even if the audience loves it, they are never *totally* satisfied: they always hope for a little bit more. After all, they've paid good money to see the show and have a night on the town.

So Bill wisely limited his live appearances. Yet throughout the sixties and seventies, never more than a few months went by without one. Most of his club material also appeared in recorded form in a series of albums.

After the success Warner Brothers had with Bill's first two albums, around the time that *I Spy* made him a nationally known star, there was even greater demand for additional records. In the fall of 1965, Bill's third album, *Why Is There Air?*, was issued. It contains some of his classic material about his childhood. He talks about the life of a kindergarten student with vivid recall. A reviewer for the *American Record Guide* commented, ''Cosby's genius for detail ought to set him to thinking about stitching his autobiography into a book or two or three. Maybe his syntax is a little wild, but when he scrutinizes, as an example, his first-grade travails, he displays all the earmarks of a Proustian observer. Consider his precise descriptions of writing around the chunks of wood imbedded in the school-issued pulp (with lines eight feet apart), the 'stick-in-the-craw' graham crackers provided by the benevolent teachers along with curdled rations of radiator-warmed milk and straws that flattened after the first suck. . . .'' The album, widely praised for its warmth and humor, rose as high as number nineteen on the hit list.

Bill's next album was *Wonderfulness*, which featured a picture of him on a go-cart (with a terrified expression) on the cover. Recorded in a live performance at Harrah's, the album covers a wide range of childhood experiences. The longest and perhaps the best cut is Bill's description of his tonsillectomy at the age of five. Again, the details are convincing and the quality of the storytelling is spellbinding. There are dramatic pauses, thoughtful asides, wonderful changes from hushed reflection to shouted urgencies. The plot—little boy has his tonsils removed—is commonplace, but the drama is enormous. Other selections on the album include a reflection about why everything Bill made in shop in high school turned into an ashtray, a comparison of the safety of a vacant lot full of broken glass and bits of metal with the dangers of playground equipment such as monkey bars and seesaws, and his recollections of the delicious terrors of horror programs on the radio. As one reviewer enthused, "Now here is an artist who can conjure up the very quiver of a five-year-old plotting escape from the bed he has been told is surrounded by a thousand poisonous snakes, who can re-create with total recall the furious inner churnings of a youth whose very life seems threatened by the lumps in his Cream of Wheat. And the wonderfulness about Cosby's talent is that he can make these poignant and precise childhood recollections so screamingly funny, so free of any taint of ickyness."

The public seemed to agree with reviewers' praise, and *Wonderfulness*, released in the late summer of 1966, rose to number seven on the album charts. At this point, all four of his albums were on the charts at the same time, and Bill's comedy albums were outselling most of the pop music of the day. That fact was dramatically underscored by the performance of his fifth album, released in May of 1967. *Revenge* rose to the number two spot on the charts, and only Herb Alpert, of all the musicians in the world, was able to outsell Bill Cosby at the record store.

Revenge epitomizes Bill Cosby's ability to re-create childhood memories—even some painful ones—and turn them into warmly funny stories that speak to the child in every listener. He talks about sibling rivalries with his younger brothers, as well as the need to be responsible for their welfare, neatly laying bare a psychological dilemma that would take a team of psychologists years to explore. He reminisces fondly about the pleasures of being scared to death by a horror movie and lingers deliciously over the frights of the walk home from the theater at night. The *American Record Guide*'s reviewer concluded, "The 'wonderfulness' of Cosby's amiable, campy, and only sporadically hilarious memories of a tender epoch defies analysis. For all I know the material may even be callously contrived, although it seems unlikely that such outlandish escapades could be wholly concocted. My own partisanship finds me greedily gobbling up every one of his yarns, and even doting on his storehouse of funny noises which emanate from the stomachs, tongues, and the very souls of children with genuine vulnerability and a shaggy fearless approach to life that smacks of verisimilitude."

One of the most interesting interviews Bill Cosby ever gave, to *Life* magazine in 1969, shed some light on the way he wrote and polished his comedy material. He was talking about a famous monologue he does about himself and his brother Russell. "The piece I do about my brother and me in bed together started out one night with me saying on stage that my brother Russell always bugged me, especially in bed. That got a laugh. So the next time I acted out a little of it. My mind was wide open, like looking through a funnel, to create and accept or reject. Then, as I acted out the roles, I brought the father into it and he talked. And I was trying to feel it and keep that funnel open. I went back and back, trying it and trying it, until it dried up. I have a piece funneling through now— some business about how people shouldn't take God's name in vain, because He's so busy with Vietnam and the race question, and by calling on Him they distract Him from His work. So I tell them I have a friend named Rudy who's not doing nothing and would be glad to help if they called on him. Just call on my friend Rudy when you want a point at the crap table. 'Oh, Rudy, please make me that hard eight!' You see?''

This approach to comedy involves a considerable risk. Unlike the comedian who fires away a barrage of one-liners, the comedian who stands up in front of an audience and "funnels" risks losing his listeners as he explores dead ends and material that may be too weak to travel far. Bill pointed out the risks himself: "What I think of as performing without a net is to start something you think is funny, and you're not sure where it's going. The way I perform I can kill a routine by entering it wrong. I won't do jokes. I do long pieces—ten, fifteen, twenty minutes. I swing out a lot, I take chances. I don't depend on a few sure things to carry me through." Bill believed that one reason

LEFT: Bill Cosby—
For Real.

RIGHT: The irre-
pressible Bill Cosby
clowns it up as
he talks about his
epic struggle with
his brother Russell
over a blanket.

ABOVE: Bill Cosby appears with Johnny Carson on *The Tonight Show*, the show that gave him his first national exposure. Note the trademark cigar in Bill's hand; he refers to them as "flesh-colored."

RIGHT: Bill and his costar Bob Culp in a tense moment from *I Spy*.

LEFT: Bill and Camille Cosby attend the Emmy Awards in 1965, when Bill won his first of three awards in a row as Best Male Performer in a Dramatic Series.

BELOW: Bill suits up to play with the Harlem Globetrotters in an exhibition game with the Boston Shamrocks. Cheering him on, at left, is Meadowlark Lemon.

ABOVE: Bill revisits the streets of Philadelphia, where he and his friends, like this group of young fans, used to play street football around the parked cars.

ABOVE: With producer/director/star Sidney Poitier, Bill made three successful movies during the 1970s. As you can tell from this photo on the set, Sidney always plays straight man to Bill's comic.

Bill Cosby rides a tricycle on the set of *Fat Albert*, his award-winning Saturday morning cartoon show that was also the basis of his doctoral thesis in education.

ABOVE: Remembering the past, Bill joins the players on Temple's football team during a game. He's wearing a Temple hat and a coach's expression.

RIGHT: These days, Bill's favorite sport is tennis. He often plays in celebrity tournaments and is known as one of the best players in show business.

Bill takes time out from rehearsals of *The Cosby Show* to go over some dialogue with Keshia Pulliam, who plays his daughter Rudy. He acts as a sort of combination coach and parent to the child actors on the show.

Bill Cosby with two of his own beautiful daughters. That's sixteen-year-old Erinn at left and eighteen-year-old Erika at right. It looks like they have Dad under control.

he was able to get away with such risks was that he had already established his likability with the audience. As he put it succinctly, "People have to like you if you're going to be a comic. After a cat establishes the fact that he's funny, forty percent of the pressure is eased up on him because, when he walks out, people already like him. As a young comic, you have to make people decide whether they like you. You have to establish that you're funny. It's then that your stuff becomes funny, because you are delivering it."

Bill's next comedy album was issued in the spring of 1968. Called *To Russell, My Brother, Whom I Slept With,* it once again mined Bill's childhood for warmth and humor. Side two is Bill at his best, in a half-hour monologue that starts out about being in bed with his brother Russell and goes on to discuss nearly every aspect of family life. The album was recorded live at a concert in Cleveland that had attracted more than ten thousand enthusiastic fans and was produced as usual by Roy Silver (this was before the breakup of Campbell Silver Cosby). Although never quite as successful as *Revenge,* this album did reach the number seven spot on the ratings charts and stayed on the charts for forty-six weeks.

By the time Bill's next comedy album was issued, in late 1968, it was possible to discern a definite shift in his choice of material. Perhaps it was because he had exhausted his ability to "funnel" back to the events of his own childhood, and possibly it was because he had already said everything he wanted to say on that subject. Whatever the reason, Bill's comedy slowly began to focus on childhood as seen, not through the eyes of the child, but through the eyes of the parent. Actually, the shift was already beginning to make itself felt even when Bill talked about his own childhood. In the early days, when Bill spoke about his father, it was in terms of "the Giant," the mysterious, willful adult who exercises complete power over a small child. In fact, the sketch that introduces "the Giant" creates a metaphor for parental power in the father's breathing, which is so strong and noisy in the little house at night that the rest of the family is literally forced to breathe in unison with the father. But by the time of the long monologue about family life in *To Russell*, the father has acquired dimensions of ordinary humanity. He demands answers from his sons and gets double-talk; he makes threats that they soon understand are empty; he gives orders in the blustering tone of a man who secretly knows that they aren't going to be followed. Bill, now a father himself, has discovered that fathers are only human.

Subsequently, Bill's comedy, although still dealing with the general area of family life, now began to see things from the parent's eyes rather than the child's. As he admitted, "Talking about my kids is part of my business, and part of how I relate to other kids, professionally and personally." So he started to talk about his wife's pregnancies, changing his daughter's diapers, trying to cope with the demands of two daughters. In short, a father's view of life. As he explained, "I think it's the little things that count when you're a daddy. Like taking your little girl for ice cream. First, you have to teach her about the concept of gravity. I can't tell you how many ice creams I've had to pick up off the floor, rinse off, and stick back on my kid's cone. Now that may sound strange, but have you bought ice cream lately? Do you know the price of ice cream? Good gosh, it's up to seventy-five cents a scoop. A *scoop*. What's in it, gold? So you can't afford to lose the bit that dribbles down the sides; each dribble's worth maybe three cents. . . ." Despite the changed point of view, his observations are as keen as ever. One reviewer commented, "His description of bath time at his house makes you wonder where he's been hiding to know so well what goes on at yours—and he makes it a little easier for all of us to chuckle about it."

Family life continued to be the staple of Bill's live comedy act as well as his albums. In an interview, Bill commented, "Some people are disappointed because I still do a family show, but if something pulls and holds a family together, and makes them laugh at themselves, that's a part of life I want to give." In another interview, he added, "It's a conscious effort on my part to stay away from anything that has to do with sex or what are known as four-letter words, unless it is to make a point. Not that I think it's bad, it's just that I'd rather work without using it."

Another thing he still preferred to work without was racially oriented material. "I don't want people laughing at the fact that I'm black and that there are white racists in the States and all over the world. So rather than make a joke about the color of my skin and the depressing fact that for three hundred years we've been used and abused, we've shuffled, danced, knelt, and prayed. I try to find a common identity with an audience. I create a situation and say, 'Hey, this happened to me and you're laughing with me about it, so can we really be so different?'" There was still some criticism, primarily from activists both black and white, of his refusal to make jokes about race, but most people in show business accepted his decision. As Sammy Davis said in Bill's defense, "Bill Cosby carries as much weight on his shoulders as any Negro I know, and he wears it as well and as lightly as any man could. He may not be a front-runner in the cause—that's not his nature—but he's totally committed. He gives freely of his time and money. In Watts, he's worked hard for community theater. The cats on the street corner dig him, and he represents something very important to me."

The fact that the cats on the street corner dug Bill Cosby was underscored in 1968 when Bill played the Apollo Theater in Harlem. *The New York Times* headline said it all: "Apollo Audience, A Tough Jury, Acquits Cosby." Bill's audience was with him all the way, not just through the routines about his childhood in the projects, a subject with which his listeners could be expected to empathize, but also through his stories about his problems in owing $833,000 in taxes and his troubles with his vintage Rolls-Royce: "It always ran so quiet, man, I didn't know it had broke down. But the trees weren't moving, so I figured it had. Then I figured maybe for $24,000, the place I was going would come to me." The Apollo crowds loved it, because they knew Bill was still talking about real life, it just happened to be the kind of reality you have to face when you're a successful entertainer.

Bill's years of experience in live comedy, combined with the kinds of risks he likes to take on the stage, had prepared him to cope with just about any kind of reception. He shared his thoughts about how to handle a live audience. "After you've established you're funny, you have to protect it. You can make the mistake of leaving stuff out of your act that people love you for. You can become hostile toward a heckler and people wonder what's happened, because you're not supposed to get angry in public. You can misread an audience. What you fear most is an audience of old people. I think we all turn more bitter the closer we come to our own death. Old people are toughest because you don't know how close to death they are upstairs. And you can be too funny. I used to want to destroy people with laughter. I wanted to make their stomachs hurt. But that isn't fair. It really hurts, and it makes people tired. So now I pace myself. I don't want people concentrating on their pain rather than their laughter. That's why they get my funniest piece at the end of the evening. Now, if the audience is just bad, I simply work faster and get it over with. Some comics will throw the kitchen sink at an unresponsive audience. Me, I don't. I'm not out there to bleed. I just figure they're dodos and get off.''

Bill's rapport with an audience is not always total. He doesn't take the drunks personally, and he's learned how to deal with the hecklers. His most serious problems come when the audience simply won't hang in with his rambling mono-logues and wait until Bill gets wherever he's going. But you have to admire him because he doesn't try to take the easy way out; he keeps developing his routines in his own style and at his own pace.

Through the late 1960s and the early 1970s, Bill continued to put out at least one comedy album a year, usually recorded live. Titles include *200 MPH*; *It's True! It's True!*; *When I Was a Kid*; *Inside the Mind*; and *My Father Confused Me . . . What Shall I Do, What Shall I Do?* Sales never again equaled those of the albums from the midsixties, but, on the other hand, the later albums always found their audience. His most successful recent album was *Bill Cosby Is Not Himself These Days, Rat Own, Rat Own, Rat Own*, which reached num-ber one hundred and stayed on the charts a total of twelve weeks. Fifteen of the albums are still in print as of this writing, and most of them still sell steadily.

Then there's the matter of the Grammy Awards.

Every year from 1964 to 1969, six straight years in a row, Bill Cosby took home the Grammy for best Comedy Album of the Year. It's an awesome domination of the field.

These days, Bill's focus has shifted away from albums, but he continues to make live appearances in the summer, when his TV series is not in production.

Chapter Nine

Time for a Change

> If you listen carefully to what a child is saying to you,
> you'll see that he has a point to make. So I listen. And
> I answer them just as seriously as possible. And if I
> don't know the answer, I'll tell them I don't know.

BILL COSBY'S SUCCESS in show business didn't make him forget his earlier dreams. In nearly every interview he gave during the late 1960s, he predicted that he would one day get his college degree and become a teacher and coach in an inner-city school. He assured reporters that in just a few years, "Boom, that's it, I have another job now, good-bye. There are too few people in the slums of the type to take a kid with a bright mind and get him to asking questions. I want to be that type." Even skeptics admitted that Bill sounded sincere . . . but they pointed out that it was one thing to think about an idea like that and another to actually put it into practice.

But events proved that Bill really did mean what he said. In 1971, he enrolled in college again, nearly ten years after he had dropped out of Temple. In fact, in the intervening decade he had raised his sights: no longer content just to get a bachelor's degree, he was going to go all the way and try for a doctorate. Bill explained to one journalist that it was all the result of an appearance he made on the campus of the University of Massachusetts (in Amherst) in the late 1960s. "After I performed at U Mass once, I started thinking and met with one of the deans, who told me I should give it a shot." Dean Dwight Allen recognized Bill's seriousness of purpose, and perhaps he also reflected on how much Bill had to give in the field of education as a result of his great rapport with children. The result was that U Mass arranged to accept him, to work out a program with flexible scheduling, and to do their best to keep the whole thing out of the media.

Of course, before Bill could get a Ph.D., he had to get that college degree he'd never completed in the 1960s. That was worked out with Temple University. He had two years of credits already, and Temple agreed to give him additional credits for courses he took at U Mass as well as for his practical experience. He received a bachelor's degree from Temple's School of Communication. That left the way clear for Bill to become a doctor of education.

It took Bill six years to complete all the necessary work for his bachelor's, master's, and doctorate. He graduated in May 1977, before an enthusiastic group of friends and family. Probably the

happiest person in the world that day was his
mother, for whom his degree was surely a dream
come true. Bill commented, "Mom just went crazy
today. She used to say, 'Education's a must.' If
she was dead, she would have gotten up to come
here today. Her tears mean so much."

Even if you're a superstar, getting a doctorate
requires the usual amount of hard work and diligent study. Bill commented, "You look at things
and you say, 'Gee whiz, this is interesting, all
these things keep popping up.' Then you find out,
gee whiz, you know, this is going to take me eight
hundred years before I'm finished with this, and
you've got to close it off. But you're enjoying it."
Bill probably also enjoyed working on his thesis.
It was called "An Integration of the Visual Media
Via *Fat Albert and The Cosby Kids* into the Elementary School Curriculum as a Teaching Aid and
Vehicle to Achieve Increased Learning." It involved the careful planning of the *Fat Albert* Saturday morning cartoon show to conform to the
best principles of teaching. In addition, Bill turned
out a series of workbooks and teacher's guides to
help adapt the *Fat Albert* shows for actual classroom use.

Bill was determined to use his education to help
others. He said firmly, "If I can keep even one
confused, unhappy kid from going down the drain,
from dropping out of school, I'll have made a real
contribution." But he had changed his mind about
exactly how he intended to accomplish his goal.
He finally accepted the fact that as Bill Cosby the

famous entertainer, he was in a position to do more to help kids than he could as Bill Cosby the good schoolteacher. The very nature of his graduate thesis emphasized the fact that he could reach millions of kids and bring them some important messages. As Bill explained, "No, I'm not going into teaching. I'm going to use my education to help teach. . . . You can be a teacher in a lot of ways. I like film and I like sound. They move the emotions. People learn from them. That's the kind of writing I want to do. Books? What's a book? Something you take down from a shelf and place on a coffee table and nobody reads it. It's not alive. Film is, and that's what I work in. . . . There are certain subjects—trigonometry, calculus, languages—that students are required to study. Most teachers don't know how to explain to a student why he's required to take these courses. The films I plan to make will explain exactly where these courses fit into the lives of the students."

Over the years, Bill evolved an educational philosophy that reflected his own experience and interests. He was most interested in reaching kids who have little other support or motivation—the kind of kids, black or white, who aren't good students, don't do their homework, flunk some of their classes, perhaps choose to drop out before they finish high school. He knew that kids like that are not likely to read books—not even their textbooks—in school. But they are interested in television and movies and radio and records, those sights and sounds that seem inherently more exciting. Why not use entertainment to help kids learn? And why limit their learning to the three Rs? Bill always believed that values and attitudes are as important as reading and writing. A kid with the right set of values can pick up a book, learning whenever he sees the need for it—just like Bill Cosby himself did. But if a kid doesn't have the right attitude, the best teachers in the world can't teach him even the fundamentals. So Bill thought that teaching vehicles ought to work on the *real* basics: teaching respect for others and for oneself; emphasizing the need to work hard to achieve important goals; stressing the values of family life, of kindness, of honesty, of helping others, of contributing to society.

When it comes right down to it, Bill's philosophy is very straight and very tough. He explains, "While these hoodlum packs are out roaming the streets and saying 'What it is, what it is' and 'Right on' and giving handshakes and challenging each other over a piece of cement that the city owns, there are some very bright ones in that group who—if they could channel themselves toward something and forget about this false manhood of 'If somebody messes with me, I'll kill him' and 'You too chicken to take a life?'—could contribute something to society. We need more involvement from parents, even if it means hitting somebody upside the head with a baseball bat to get them to realize that even though school is not what everyone would like it to be and that other schools have better books or whatever it is, it is now up to us to make the most out of the old torn ones. I don't want to get into anybody's business, or make it sound like Bill Cosby—who makes X number of hundreds of thousands of dollars—is going to tell the lady on welfare, who's got a side job and three boys living down wherever, how to run her home. But I'm saying that, philosophically, most of those children want somebody to tell them how to go, and if we can get these children to have love and respect for their parents, perhaps they will do the turnaround themselves."

Bill's continuing commitment to education was manifested by his choice of professional projects. *Fat Albert,* with its team of academic consultants and its effort to teach good values and moral principles, was an important part of that commitment. Another was Bill's decision to appear as a regular on *The Electric Company,* the educational program for grade-school children produced by The Children's Television Workshop, the creators of *Sesame Street. The Electric Company* was intended to be more serious and more academically oriented than *Sesame Street,* and to reach older kids. It would teach reading, phonics, and the basics of math. For several years in the 1970s, Bill Cosby was one of the "big kids" on the program, doing skits that involved the sounds of words or the difference in vowel sounds. It was a bit limiting for Bill's classic approach to comedy, but he enjoyed the work, and he knew it was important.

"Teaching kids and providing a good example for them is very important, meaningful to me. I love being around them, and I feel I gain as much from them as they hopefully learn from me—I am a lucky man."

One conclusion Bill Cosby was certain of: 'The most important educational vehicle in all life is a parent figure." He knew how much his mother had given him, how much of his own determination, and his success as well, was due to her early teaching about the value of education and pride in achievement. So Bill was determined to offer his own children the same things he had gotten from his mother. He says that one reason he decided to go on and get a doctorate was to show his children that their father could do something more than just tell funny stories. "I feel that school, achieving the education and going higher, is something that I wanted to do for myself, and also to show my children that, although their father does one thing, it's possible to do many things; that human beings have a brain that is capable of doing three or four things at one time. And also that things are not 'all that hard,' as long as someone is there to explain it to you, and we should not be afraid of those things."

His concern for the quality of his children's lives, along with the demands of his enrollment in graduate school at U Mass, brought a major change to the Cosby family: a move from Los Angeles to a farmhouse outside Amherst. The house Bill and Camille chose was a 135-year-old structure which they have renovated and decorated with comfortable country antiques. Set on 286 acres, there is also a tennis court and two barns; one is Bill's office and the other is a permanent guest house for Mrs. Anna Cosby. The idea was to provide the Cosby children with secure roots and a life-style uncontaminated by their father's celebrity.

The Cosby family lives much like any other prosperous family in that area. Camille drives the kids to school in the morning, does the marketing, and fixes the family meals. She is happy in their home in Massachusetts. "I love it here because I am not an extrovert. There's not a lot of people driving by and bothering us. I never did get used to all the sightseers. Sudden success is very difficult to deal with. All of a sudden you're known, and people ask you to do all kinds of things. But Bill has learned to say no." Bill these days is more likely to say no to certain professional oportunities because he hates to leave home. He enjoys a place "where there's land for your children; where time doesn't play such a great part in what you do, where people tend to trust a little more." The move seems to have been good for the Cosby children, too. Bill complained that his son Ennis's grades were getting to be so good that Bill was afraid he was losing one of his major sources of new comedy material!

Since the move to Massachusetts and his return to the field of education, Bill seems more at peace with himself. Doing what he really wants to do, what he really believes in, makes him happier and gives him more patience with the demands of a career in show business. As Camille noted, it's always hard to handle sudden celebrity. And although Bill did better than most, the strain was sometimes visible. Critics were quick to comment on it. For example, syndicated entertainment columnist Dan Lewis said, "In recent years, I was not that impressed with Cosby. The sparkle seemed to be missing, and Cosby emerged as an angry man, rather than the smooth-working, refreshing young comic. . . . I remember a press conference in Las Vegas several years ago, when seventy TV editors and columnists left fuming at his condescending attitude."

Bill Cosby himself talked about his anger. In an interview with James Spina, he talked about what he saw as the unfairness of the interview process. "I used to get really worried about what I was going to say, but it never really matters. This guy who has never seen the sun wanders up to your hotel room. Maybe he is like Earl Wilson and he orders this floppy sandwich with a pickle. In between gulping down his free lunch, it's 'Gumble mulch gulp?' for a question, and it doesn't matter what I say because he is going to write down what he thinks I should have said anyway. Or maybe the cat is like Rex Reed, who'll scribble down that Cosby said, 'Hey, baby' and 'baby this' and 'baby that.' Listen, Rex, don't sprinkle my talk with 'baby.' Maybe that's Godfrey Cambridge, but not me. Don't just lump us all together."

Most revealing of Bill's attitude during those

years when he was coming to terms with stardom was a short story he wrote for *Playboy* in 1971, called "This One Will Kill You." It's about "the world's most fantastic comedian back in the year 2070," Edwin Duff. Edwin is making $3 million a night . . . but he has to give 73 percent of it to his agent, Howie. A sharp dig at those who leech on the talented: Edwin says he doesn't mind giving Howie that cut because, "After all, it was Howie who told him never to wear a brown suit onstage; that advice had easily been the turning point in Edwin's illustrious career." The story continues in Edwin's dressing room backstage. An old woman appears and asks why he didn't answer the note she wrote him twenty years ago. As Edwin tries to answer, she pulls out a knife and stabs him through the heart. "Edwin, a little embarrassed and in pain, just stood there, a small smile on his face, trying to show them how weary he was, hoping the woman and her husband would allow him to rest—maybe later he'd be able to give them more time and a better explanation. Perhaps he'd take them out to dinner."

Things in the dressing room go from bad to worse. A backslapping politician manages to drive the knife deeper into Edwin's heart; then a souvenir-seeking teenager slices off both his ears. As Edwin collapses and dies, he hears nothing but the constant demands: drive me home, sign this for my mother, take a year's subscription, tell me why you didn't answer the note, remember the man in Miami who says he knows you. . . . The story is a dark view of the demands made on a public figure, and at that point in Bill's life, they must have seemed threatening to his psychological existence if not his physical safety.

Leaving Hollywood and moving to the quiet of the country was perhaps an act of self-preservation. Eventually, it enabled Bill to put things back in perspective. As he put it, "You get a big public image and people—old friends, even—think of you as something sacred and unapproachable, Mister Cosby or whatever it is. But inside, we don't think that way about ourselves at all. Pretty much the contrary. With all the money I make, and however successful Mister Bill Cosby is in his career, to my real self I'm just old Shorty, and that's all I'll ever be."

Chapter Ten

From the Little Screen to the Big One

> Say I have a million and a half in the bank. No reason why I couldn't back a couple of $500,000 pictures—if I believe in them. Risky business? Sure it is. But this is what I want to do, and my wife is willing to go along with me on this. She knows how important it is to me. I think of all those cats whose dreams will die unless I help them.

LIKE MANY OTHER STARS whose fame has come from television, Bill Cosby was suddenly offered movie roles in abundance. Everyone hopes that popularity on the small screen of TV can be transferred to the large screen of movie theaters. But frequently this assumption is ill founded; just ask Henry Winkler or Farrah Fawcett or Suzanne Somers. Some people say the reason is that television stardom calls for a low-key, relaxed, intimate sort of appeal that is simply too diluted when it arrives on the silver screen. Others suggest it is because television stars are so anxious to break out of the mold of their series character that they choose their movie roles unwisely, portraying characters that do not suit them physically or emotionally. Still others, less kind, assert that it's a matter of talent and experience: television stars are simply professional lightweights.

Whatever the reason, the rate of failure for TV stars in movies is alarming. So Bill Cosby thought the matter over carefully before he made any decision. He felt it wouldn't do his career any particular good to play the same sort of character he made famous in *I Spy*, although he certainly had plenty of offers to play that type of role. He wanted to do something different, but he wanted to stay within the bounds of good taste and continue to reach a family audience, as he had through his TV shows and personal appearances. The format he finally settled on was a western.

A *western*? you ask in surprise. That's just what all the major studios said when Bill made the rounds looking for financing and distribution. His own production company, Jemmin Productions, initiated the project, with a script that centered on the struggles of a black family on the western frontier. Most of the studio executives Bill talked to were either bored or scornful. It was obvious that they were not interested in making a picture that focused so specifically on blacks, nor were they captivated by the family-interest angle. To them, a western was a bunch of white guys shooting up the town and everyone in it. Bill's sensitive script (written by Harry Essex and Oscar Saul) about a father and son searching for the son's horse and encountering both a black outlaw and a vicious white sheriff, was turned down all over Hollywood.

But Bill knew his script was authentic history: "We integrated our towns because that's the way it was. The West was a place for bust-outs of all types and colors, people who were down on their luck." And he was convinced that there was an eager market for films that the whole family could see together. "GP pictures only . . . and not just because that's what I believe in. It's good business, too. That Walt Disney was the slickest guy who ever operated in this town. Do you realize that for every three people who see a Disney picture, there are probably two who didn't really want to come to the theater? That's right. Parents go because that's something their kid can see. And maybe not just once, but two or three times. Man, when you got one or two out of every three people going to the theater when they don't even want to be there, you got something going for you."

It was Camille Cosby who urged Bill to make the film even though he had no studio backing. She put it to him this way: "If you believe enough in the picture, why don't you go ahead and put the money in it?" Bill, against all expert advice, agreed.

The picture started shooting in the fall of 1971. Jemmin Productions had its star, a script, a location in Scottsdale, Arizona, a good supporting cast that included Yaphet Kotto, Gloria Foster, Leif Erickson, and Douglas Turner Ward; most important of all, it also had $350,000 of Bill Cosby's money. The producer was Marvin Miller, who had produced many of Bill's television specials as well as one of his series. Bill and Marvin both took deferred salaries to hold the costs down during production, and they decided they would just begin, and go on shooting as long as the money held out. Luckily, before that happened, they found an independent investor, a California mobile-home builder named John Crean. The final budget was in the neighborhood of $800,000, and the film was finished one week ahead of schedule.

Just before the film, entitled *Man and Boy*, was released, Bill Cosby talked about it to Hollywood columnist Bob Thomas. "I can honestly say that this has been the most stimulating, the best thing I have ever been associated with. . . . I am convinced it is going to be a winner." To another journalist he cracked that the only nude in the picture was the horse. He also told the press that this was only the first of many family-oriented pictures he intended to do, and that he wanted to put increasing emphasis on the educational aspects of his films as well as the entertainment value.

Unfortunately, this was a project where the intentions were better than the execution. Reviews were no better than lukewarm. *The New York Times* said, "The plight of a black man in the frontier West is a wonderfully provocative film theme. As the star and engineer of an admirably economic project, *Man and Boy*, which genuinely tries to say something worthwhile, Bill Cosby is to be commended. If only the picture were better. . . . The movie is a slack, meandering affair, badly needing unified bite and impact. And the direction of E.W. Swackhamer is no help at all. . . . Pulled together taut and hard, along with some good cutting dialogue, the film might have scored a neat home run. But at least it puts Mr. Cosby on first base in screen drama." *Cue* called the picture disappointing and blamed the director for handling the material "clumsily and lethargically, dissipating any emotional impact." Cosby's own performance was termed "fine" and "effective."

When the picture was released in the spring of 1972, it seemed that the audiences agreed with the critics. Its performance at the box office was modest. Only the fact that the movie had cost so little to make kept it from being a financial disaster.

Despite the lack of success with his first venture, Bill was ready to plunge into a second one. This time, it was for another cause he believed in deeply—friendship. A major studio had bought a script written by Walter Hill about two seedy private eyes in Los Angeles, and they sent it to Bill to read. He said he would do the film on one condition: that his friend Bob Culp be allowed to direct. Culp, who had also been sent the script, made the same demand. The studio's answer was no; the stars' response was to buy the rights to the script themselves.

Once again, the first order of business was to try to raise money to make the film. Once again, none of the major studios were interested. Eventually, Bob and Bill found an investor in an old friend. Cinematographer Fouad Said had been the cameraman for the *I Spy* series. Since leaving the show, he had built up a multimillion-dollar business called

Cinemobile, which moved studio sets from one location to another. He agreed to put up the money for their tightly budgeted film, and Bob Culp finally had his chance to direct a film.

Bob explained the basic concept of the film. "Hickey and Boggs have no money, can't pay their rent, their business phone has been cut off, and they use telephone booths for their office. They are far from glamorous, unlike the private detectives in old movies. On a routine missing-persons assignment, they stumble over several dead bodies. There is a fantastic amount of money involved, which they know nothing about. They can't find anybody, they don't know who anybody is, or what it's all about." This plot summary alone indicates some of the difficulties facing director Culp. As he described it, "I put the thing together like a jigsaw puzzle. I fill in one space, and the audience will have to use its imagination to fill in two spaces. Altogether, it's like a well-assembled mystery novel."

Bill was happy to be working with his friend once again, and he liked the idea of teaming up with Bob to portray the mirror image of their characters in *I Spy*. His role of Hickey was an ex-cop with a good sense of humor and a bad marriage. Instead of playing a Rhodes scholar with an incredible fund of information, he was playing a slow thinker who was continually mystified by the new developments in the case. It was obvious that he got a kick out of the reversal of his image.

What was also becoming increasingly obvious

was that the movie Bill Cosby and Bob Culp really wanted to make was not the one Walter Hill had written. Hill was a specialist in a certain kind of action-packed, violent film that nevertheless had interesting character development; among his works have been the screenplays for *The Getaway*, a Charles Bronson adventure, and more recently, the Eddie Murphy hit, *48 Hours*. Bob and Bill liked the character development, but they didn't especially care for the violence. Perhaps because the director never succeeded in resolving the conflict between the script and the picture he wanted to make, the film itself never quite succeeds, either. The plot has so many unexplained twists that it is extremely difficult to follow, and the characters never really come alive, since their development is continually interrupted by a shootout.

Reviews of *Hickey and Boggs* were mixed. *Take One*'s reviewer complained that "the plot is never all that clear" but went on to add that "the film more than makes up for that with two fine characterizations by the leads, some great photography, and an awful lot of action. *The New York Times*' A. H. Weiler began his review by saying, "Although they've clicked as the supercool, funny, and compatible black-white team of international sleuths in TV's *I Spy* series, Bill Cosby and Bob Culp are a good deal less convincing as the seedy private eyes of *Hickey and Boggs*," and concluded, "As antiheroes, both Mr. Culp and Mr. Cosby are serious, sullen, and extremely laconic. Terse passes at dialogue merely indicate their personal relationships and their concomitant, bloody, thankless mission.''

Released in the fall of 1972, the film was not a success at the box office. Competing with such movies as *Dirty Harry* and *The Godfather*, films that were comfortable with a high level of violence, *Hickey and Boggs* fell between the cracks: not violent enough for action-film fans, and not strong enough to stand on its own without the stimulus of the action.

Perhaps the fate of his first two films made Bill Cosby realize how difficult it can be for the novice to succeed in making movies, or perhaps he thought he could use the experience of working for other filmmakers. Whatever the reason, the rest of his movie career to date has not involved him behind the scenes, only in front of the camera.

His next movie appearance, and one of his most successful, was in a film that was produced and directed by his costar, friend Sidney Poitier. The film was *Uptown Saturday Night*, and the year it was released, 1974, was also the year that marked Poitier's twenty-fifth anniversary in films. A practiced pro, he had already appeared in *For the Love of Ivy, To Sir with Love, Lilies of the Field,* and *Guess Who's Coming to Dinner?*; he had two Oscar nominations and one win. Poitier's extensive experience in the film business enabled him to do what Bill Cosby had tried to do in his own venture with Jemmin Productions: make a film with and about blacks.

Uptown Saturday Night had a truly all-star cast.

In addition to leads Poitier and Cosby, the film featured Harry Belafonte, Flip Wilson, Richard Pryor, Roscoe Lee Browne, and Calvin Lockhart. Female leads included Rosalind Cash (who was also in *Hickey and Boggs*), Paula Kelly, and Ketty Lester. It was produced by Poitier for his own production company, Verdon, and distributed by Warner Brothers. In addition to the blacks who were working in front of the camera, at least a quarter of the crew and production team were also black.

The movie was intended to be nothing more than an evening of entertainment for the audience. The plot revolved around two buddies who are robbed in an after-hours club; a gang of thugs come in and relieve cabdriver Cosby of his ill-gotten gains and factory worker Poitier of his winning lottery ticket. They team up to recover their valuables; as the press release summary puts it, ''The amateur detective work of Poitier and Cosby takes them through the ghetto areas of an industrial city and brings them face-to-face with various dangers and threats, results in their being beaten by bandits, cheated out of their money by Pryor, getting in Dutch with their wives, meeting gang leaders in the church where Wilson preaches, getting involved in the various games of a church picnic, finally trapping Lockhart, leaping ninety feet from a bridge into a river in an effort to retrieve a suitcase containing their valuables, and winding up in a hospital—beaten and broken, but smiling. They've gotten the goods back.''

The story line of *Uptown Saturday Night* was one that Bill Cosby could feel more comfortable with than he did with *Hickey and Boggs*. There was a lot of action, but the level of realism was that of a cartoon. Like Wile E. Coyote or Sylvester the Cat, Bill and Sidney bounced back from every defeat, smiling and more or less intact. Not even the bad guys really got hurt. It was intended to be a sort of fantasy, the kind of daydream two working stiffs might indulge in over a couple of drinks at the end of a long, hard week.

Of course, the movie was also very funny. How could it miss, with Cosby, Wilson, and Pryor on hand? The humor was interwoven with the plot at every turn, and it was well written and brilliantly performed. Vincent Canby commented, ''*Uptown Saturday Night* is an exuberant black joke that utilizes many of the stereotypical attitudes that only black writers, directors, and actors can decently get away with. You've never seen so much eye-popping fear and unwarranted braggadocio used in the service of laughs. Yet the result is not a put-down comedy but a cheerful jape that has the effect of liberating all of us from our hang-ups.''

Released in the summer of 1974, the movie was an immediate hit—and not just with black audiences. The teenagers, who comprise the bulk of summertime audiences, enjoyed the blend of comedy and action, and the fact that most of the cast was black merely made the movie seem ''hip.'' Reviews were good, and box office receipts were even better. *Uptown Saturday Night* was a success by any definition.

Bill Cosby was generally singled out by reviewers for his excellent performance in the film. Unfortunately, he was also singled out by critics of the film's advertising campaign. Warner Brothers' ad agency made three radio spots for the movie using Bill Cosby, and one of them drew a lot of flak. It featured Bill, with that warm voice and that humorous inflection; the script read, "Hi, this is Bill Cosby. Remember the good old days when you used to go uptown to Harlem and have a good time—before it became very, very dangerous? Well, you can still go uptown without getting your head beat in, by going downtown to see *Uptown Saturday Night*. This way, the people are all on the screen and won't jump off and clean your head out. . . ."

When the commercial was aired, many blacks were irate. It seemed to play right into the unfavorable stereotypes they were trying to defeat, to be a put-down both of Harlem in particular and black people in general. Protests were lodged with CORE, NAACP, the Urban League, and the FCC. There were editorials in black newspapers and even a few picketers. And Bill Cosby was placed squarely in the center of the controversy.

He was out of the country at the time, making appearances in Europe, and he wisely made no comment. Viewed from the perspective of ten years later, it seems evident that the commercial was merely intended to be funny in the same way the movie was—by audaciously using black stereotypes as a source of comedy, inviting audiences to laugh at the ridiculousness of the exaggerations. At worst, it was an error of judgment not to realize that without the context the movie managed to establish, a fifteen-second radio spot might be misinterpreted. In the long run, it proved to be a tempest in a teapot: Bill Cosby's life and work make it clear that he was not the sort of man to cast slurs on black people or black neighborhoods.

The success of *Uptown Saturday Night* encouraged Sidney Poitier to make a second film of much the same sort. Called *Let's Do It Again*, it had a plot that once again involved two innocents who end up taking on a variety of crooks and con men. This time, Poitier and Cosby are members of a lodge that is trying to raise money. They borrow some cash from the lodge's building fund and add some money of their own, then set out on an adventure to New Orleans to increase their stake through betting on the fights. They do so unexpectedly well that they are soon the target of the local mob. After a lot of action and many laughs along the way, they end up accomplishing their goal for the lodge and triumphing over the bad guys.

Other than the two leads, the only actor from the first film to appear in the second one was Calvin Lockhart, this time playing a New Orleans gangster. New faces included actor Ossie Davis and two television stars, John Amos and Jimmie Walker of *Good Times*.

Bill enjoyed making movies when he had no responsibilities other than appearing in front of the camera. He commented that he was able to get more sleep than he usually did and spend more time with his family, and that was one of the major reasons for taking on the assignment. He downplayed the financial gain. "I'm getting $75,000 and ten percent of the gross for this, and Sidney has me grounded. No airplanes until the picture is complete. That means I can't go anywhere, take any bookings for ten weeks. You know what I could be making in ten weeks of club and college dates? Five hundred thousand dollars. And I'm doing this for $75,000. So I'm not here for the money. It's fun. Even though I work hard around here, and play my part professionally and well—I'm right on it when I'm supposed to be—this is like a vacation."

Many people thought that the sense of fun that pervaded the set made it onto the screen. The chemistry between Sidney as the straight man and Bill as the comedian had improved with practice, and they really made a winning team. There was also much praise for Bill's acting. *The New York Times*' critic Richard Eder said, "The movie's main strength is Bill Cosby, who looks like a starved sheep in wolf's clothing, and is shifty and woebegone at the same time. Mr. Cosby, wearing a tangerine suit with Bermuda shorts and pink sunglasses to impersonate a major mobster, is hilarious; even better is his line, barked over a telephone to impress a minor mobster: 'I understand you're six feet two and good-looking. How would you like to be four feet two and ugly?' ''

The film did well at the box office, although not quite as well as its predecessor, and it made Bill Cosby more viable as a movie actor. At about the time Bill was receiving good reviews for *Let's Do It Again*, he signed for a lead role in the Twentieth Century-Fox production, *Mother, Jugs & Speed*. It starred Bill as Mother, Raquel Welch as Jugs, and Harvey Keitel as Speed.

A movie of very little merit made it to the screen, but there are indications that it started out with creditable artistic ambitions. The screenplay was written by Tom Mankiewicz, who had two successful James Bond flicks to his credit; the film was directed and coproduced by Peter Yates, who had directed Steve McQueen in *Bullitt*. The initial story seemed to have been a dark comedy about the reality behind the façade of the ambulance business. Far from being dedicated Samaritans, the employees are mostly cynical and uncaring, and the trio of leading characters obviously provides numerous opportunities for deathbed humor. But somewhere along the line, the humor turned from black to exploitative.

Reviewer Vincent Canby put his finger squarely on the weakness of the film. ''*Mother, Jugs & Speed*, a comedy about a supremely schlocky private ambulance service in Los Angeles, begins with a great deal of promise. Playing the president of F&B Ambulance Company, Allen Garfield, who is to the interpretation of American seediness what

Laurence Olivier is to Shakespeare, is giving a pep talk to his drivers. He is drawing a moving portrait of an America on the brink of despair. There are no more frontiers, he says in effect. Inflation, unemployment, and the general economic depression have sapped the strength of this great nation we all know and love. He pauses for dramatic effect. Then, though it may only be something he ate, hope seems to flicker in his bloodshot eyes. He smiles with sudden enthusiasm. 'But,' he says, 'thanks to muggings, malnutrition, and disease, we still have a chance to make a buck!' If the movie had more of his deviousness, paranoia, and consistently rotten charm, it might have been a most original—and terrifying—comedy. As directed by Peter Yates and written by Tom Mankiewicz, the film comes across as a rude-joke Valentine. . . .''

Other reviewers agreed in panning the film. In an effort to attract viewers despite the dismal things they had read or heard about the film, Twentieth Century-Fox mounted a tacky promotional campaign. Instructions to theater owners suggested using ambulances as publicity gimmicks and concluded forthrightly, ''Send your mercy van tooling through town, putting a well-endowed young lady—in a T-shirt emblazoned JUGS—behind the wheel.'' The result of such creative thinking was embarrassment for all concerned—and no added interest at the box office.

Bill Cosby's next film was again with Sidney Poitier.

The particular subject Poitier wanted to tackle

was one in which Bill Cosby also had a special interest: how to help young people in disadvantaged neighborhoods not only survive but come out pointed toward success. The movie was called *A Piece of the Action*, and the plot revolves around two "lovable crooks" who are blackmailed by a policeman played by James Earl Jones, into going straight and helping the kids in their community. Poitier's responsibility is to teach the youngsters how to cope with the world, and Cosby's is to find them jobs once Poitier thinks they are ready. There is a certain amount of overt pedagogy in the movie, some scenes in which Poitier is actually telling the viewers just what it will take for them to get a piece of the action.

Film critic Bernard Drew complained, "*A Piece of the Action* isn't a movie at all, but an illustrated lecture, a polemic to young black people advising them that if they want to get on in the white world, they had better mind their manners, no matter what they really feel or think. . . ."

Most of the entertainment in the film came from costar Bill Cosby. *After Dark*'s reviewer commented, "Cosby has style and great timing, and the scene in which he comes on to the youth center's director (played by the stunningly beautiful Denise Nicholas) . . . is a classic bit of comedy." In general, Cosby's reviews were better than those of the film, which *The New York Times* called a "candy-coated training film." It was reasonably successful at the box office in the neighborhoods where Poitier's "constituency" was to be found, but was less popular than the previous two films with the general public. When it comes to the movie business, good intentions are rarely enough.

In 1978, Bill Cosby appeared in one more movie, his most recent screen role to date. It was the star-studded *California Suite*, based on the Neil Simon play. The movie was actually four different stories, connected only by the fact that they all take place in the same suite of the Beverly Hills Hotel. Other stars included Alan Alda, Jane Fonda, Michael Caine, Maggie Smith, Walter Matthau, and Elaine May. Bill's segment dealt with the vacation of two black doctors from Chicago who bring their wives to California for a week of sun and fun that rapidly turns into a nightmare of comic complications: flat tires, faulty plumbing, tennis injuries . . . and so on.

Bill's fellow sufferer amid all this disaster was played by Richard Pryor, and the two of them had a field day, egging each other on to bigger and better displays of temper and moans of despair. Director Herbert Ross allowed a slightly frantic atmosphere to increase as the segment moved on, and many reviewers thought the slapstick was a bit too broad by the end of the film. But there were some wonderful moments along the way, vintage Bill Cosby. Unfortunately, most reviewers passed over this highly comic segment to focus on the more dramatic performances of Jane Fonda, Maggie Smith, Alan Alda, and Michael Caine; Cosby and Pryor got a little bit lost in the shuffle.

Perhaps the most important aspect of that segment in *California Suite* was that it served as Bill's first rehearsal for a character—an upper-middle-class black doctor—that was later to provide him with the biggest hit of his career.

Chapter Eleven

A Triumphant Return to Television

> The show is an extension of my real life but also of my stand-up comedy. Fat Albert is an extension of things I made up about my childhood. The Huxtable family is an extension of a monologue on my life as a father.

IN THE SUMMER OF 1984, Bill Cosby announced that he had signed with NBC—the network that had carried the show that first made him a national success, *I Spy*—to do a new series for their fall schedule.

Veteran observers were surprised by the announcement, since after the quick demise of his last show, in 1976, Bill had vowed never to do another series, claiming he felt he had nothing left to offer series television. What changed his mind? Basically, it was his dissatisfaction with the current programming on TV. He joked that it was cheaper to do a show than to throw out all six of his television sets.

More seriously, he explained his point of view. "About four years ago I was home one night, and about midnight Camille went to bed. I decided to stay up and watch what was on cable. That night I saw three movies about rape. They all seemed designed to do the same thing—show women having their clothes torn off, show the violence of a man taking a woman, show a woman screaming for help. The next night I watched again. This time I heard people cursing for no reason other than to get a laugh. Once more, the woman was never shown doing anything practical, never demonstrating she could get along in life without a man. Next, I began to monitor the networks and the independent stations: women degraded, cops-and-robbers shows with the guns getting bigger and bigger, cars going for a half block on two wheels and then crashing, the women in scanty clothes as only the hors d'oeuvres for the male hero. I'm not a Puritan, but as a concerned parent I began to ask, 'Where is Carol Burnett when I need her? Where is Lucille Ball?' ''

With Camille's encouragement, Bill began to develop ideas for a new show, and eventually he came up with the idea of a regular family sit-com . . . except for the fact that the regular family happened to be black. In many respects, the concept was like one he had advanced fifteen years earlier. He said then he'd like to do a show about a black family that just went through ordinary life, living next door to some Mr. Average played by Jack Lemmon, making no big deal of its blackness. Finally, he got the chance to make exactly that kind of a show.

Bill plays the role of Dr. Heathcliff Huxtable, an obstetrician-gynecologist who is committed to his line of work and has five children of his own to prove it. He is married to Clair, a lovely lawyer, played by Phylicia Ayers-Allen, the talented sister of dancer/actress Debbie Allen. They have a comfortable house, and their children range in age from five-year-old Rudy to a daughter away at college.

Bill explained, "If this were 1964, my wife could do the cooking and I could be the guy on the sofa who just says, 'Let your mother handle this.' But today a lot of things have changed—and I want the show to reflect those changes. A family where the father cooks, too, and pitches in with the kids, and where everyone has responsibilities." He added, "We're talking about a program that hopefully will be going into millions and millions of homes. And I feel a great responsibility to make it as good—and as real—as I can."

It's no secret that Bill's own family has provided a lot of the reality for *The Cosby Show*. Kathleen Fury, writing for *TV Guide*, pointed out the obvious similarities: "The parallels between the real and the television Cosby families are several. Cliff has five children; so does Cosby. In both families, there's just one son. Both families have a daughter with a gender-neutral name. The names of his TV wife (Clair) and his real wife (Camille) both begin with C, which is probably no coincidence to a man who gave all five of his

children names beginning with E. And both Cosby
and his character are successful, well-educated black
men who speak out for such old-fashioned values
as family life, education, and commitment in
marriage.''

In fact, the similarities run even deeper. Many
of the events on the show come from events in the
Cosby family. Bill reveals, ''A pet goldfish dies
and I have to explain about death to my youngest
daughter. My son Ennis tells me he doesn't want
to be a professional, 'just regular people,' and I
have to persuade him that 'just regular people'
have their problems, too. I tell him things like,
regular people don't have maids to clean their
rooms and do their laundry, so he'd better start
doing those things himself. These fragmentary ideas
become shows. In this series, you can take two
lines of truth and write twenty-four minutes of
script based on them.'' He went on to give another
example. ''When my son Ennis is infatuated with
a girl, he'll put on ten tons of cologne and bathe
maybe seven times a day. The writer of the script,
Matt Robinson, has a son who came home one day
with his ears pierced and an earring in one of
them. This led to a show pointing up the crazy
lengths a teenage boy will go to in order to impress a girl. In the script, I chastise my son, and
then I tell my father how dumb the boy is for
doing that. Then my father tells the crazy things *I*
did—and then my mother tells on *him*. Universal
truths, recognizable by everyone.''

Bill and Carsey-Werner, the production company he was working with, came up with a short presentation film, featuring Cliff Huxtable discussing sex problems with his daughters. They took the tape to NBC. Both Grant Tinker, the president of the network, and Brandon Tartikoff, head of programming, were interested. Tartikoff liked the tape, and he remembered having seen Bill recently on Johnny Carson's show discussing much the same thing about his own daughters. After a bit of preliminary testing, NBC ordered a minimum of seven shows for the fall 1984 season.

One of Bill's conditions for doing the show was that it be shot in New York, much closer to home than the West Coast. It was decided to produce the show at NBC's Brooklyn studio—once the site of the old Vitagraph silent film stages. It's in a comfortable low-key neighborhood, where cast and crew can eat in the local coffee shops without being hassled. According to the owner of a bagel bakery in the area, Bill's own special passion is a huge bagel with ham and swiss on the top, decorated with lettuce and tomato. Bill's home for the duration is a rented Manhattan townhouse. The show is taped on Thursday nights, starting at seven P.M., usually finishing around eleven. So Bill is sometimes able to get back to Massachusetts for the weekend.

According to people who have watched the show in progress, there's no question about who's in charge of *The Cosby Show*. Not only does Bill come up with the concept for many of the shows, he's the one who shapes and refines the script

during rehearsals, sending writers back to the drawing board to capture reality more convincingly.
He's also the one who coaches the young actors
who play the Huxtable children, helping them learn
to act more like real children and less like the
children ordinarily seen on family sit-coms. Malcolm-Jamal Warner, who plays son Theo, says
Bill helped him after he blew his first audition by
making Theo come on too strong. "I played Theo
as a real rebellious kid. Mr. C. said, 'Would you
really talk to your father like that?' I said no, and
he said, 'Well, how would you talk to your dad?'
So I worked on it, and the second time I read, I
acted more natural, didn't talk back. And I got the
part!" The boy went on to explain what it was like
to work with Bill Cosby: "Mr. C. is so much like
my real dad. And that helps me play Theo better,
because the whole thing feels like my real family.
And I believe the reason our show works so well is
because Mr. C. has drawn on his real-life family
for situations and is like a parent to us kids off-
screen, so it's easy for us to play our roles convincingly. He deals with us so realistically because
his own kids are just like us. Maybe that's why he
wanted us to meet them—so we could relate better
to him."

Insiders all comment on the real family atmo-
sphere that has been established on the set of *The
Cosby Show*. The actress who plays Clair Huxtable,
Phylicia Ayers-Allen, says, "We became like a
family when we shot the pilot." The mother of
Tempestt Bledsoe, the nine-year-old who plays

daughter Vanessa, comments, "When the kids make mistakes during taping, Bill is sometimes hard on them. But they never take it in the wrong way, because he treats them as a father would, with tons of love behind the discipline." A journalist visiting the set noticed an example. "When one of his TV children knocks a picture off an end table, he says, 'You've been walking by that table for two weeks now. You blind?' But it's said matter-of-factly, not in anger, and the next time around the child actor watches where she's going." And Malcolm-Jamal gives another example of Cosby's paternalism on the set. "One time we were taping and Keshia Pulliam (the six-year-old who plays Rudy) came around a corner and bumped right into Mr. C. It was so sudden it scared her, and she started crying. Mr. C. stopped the taping for about five minutes, then said, 'Let's do it again.' But Keshia was still a little sad—so this time when she came around the corner, Mr. C. got down on the floor and started crying. Keshia started laughing and felt a lot better."

Bill Cosby was very clear about his goal when he set out to do this new series. "I want to show a family like the kind I know: children who are almost a pain in the neck, and parents who aren't far behind. A husband and wife who have their moments of love, smiles, anger, of not really liking each other, and it's sort of real. And it isn't a question of either you love me or you don't." After the first episodes were taped, Bill felt he had achieved what he'd set out to do. "I hardly ever watch my work, but with this show it's different. I watch every week. And at the end of every segment, I find myself with a smile on my face, because I really like that family and the feeling they give me."

That's a feeling Bill shares with millions of other viewers. *The Cosby Show* attracted a large audience from the start, and with nearly every week of the 1984–85 season, it grew. By the end of the season, the show had reached the coveted number one spot in the ratings. It won the People's Choice Award for top television comedy, and it was nominated for an Emmy.

The reviewers were as enthusiastic as the audiences. *Cue* predicted, "*The Cosby Show* looks like a winner. . . ." *TV Guide*'s Robert MacKenzie said, "All the Cosby themes are percolating in this NBC series, and some of the writing seems to show his touch. His deadpan acting style has reached perfection. In my view, this is the best new show of the season. . . ." *The New York Times* said, "This particular family happens to be black, but its life-style and problems are universal middle class. The difference is simply that Mr. Cosby, here at his very best, can take the ordinary and make it seem delightfully fresh. He is not just another harassed father. He is the ultimate father dealing with problems that are terribly and hilariously real. . . . With only the premier to go on, *The Cosby Show* is by far the classiest and most entertaining situation comedy of the season."

When you stop to think about it, the show really

does seem like the culmination of Bill's career as
an entertainer. It is family-oriented, like most of
Bill's material over the years. It teaches moral
behavior and good values through entertainment. It
portrays real life, the kind Bill had been observing
for years and using as material in his comedy
routines. Not only does Bill check the scripts for
that characteristic, he even has a behavioral scien-
tist to help him get it right. And he has succeeded
in portraying a black family as representative of
universal middle-class attitudes and values.

Media critic Tom Carson analyzed this success
in a long article in the *Village Voice*. "*The Cosby
Show* embodies both its star's assumptions of equal
access to the dominant culture's values and his
pointed insistence on partaking of the most status-
oriented of that culture's goodies. This family isn't
only well off, but affluent—they may boast the
largest, most tastefully decorated home in sit-com
history. Cosby's character isn't just unparticularized
white-collar, like most sit-com fathers—he's a doctor, specifically an obstetrician-gynecologist. This
family, quite determinedly, isn't black in anything
but their skin color. I don't mean just in their
life-style—even their cultural background, and their
whole context of reference, is that of American
Caucasians. The show's utter traditionalism is another way for Cosby to stake his own claim to a
white franchise—he's going to go all the way back
to *Father Knows Best* and do it better than Robert
Young ever did."

Carson may be overstating the case. In fact, the

Huxtable family life-style is much like that of many black professionals. The enjoyment of the material rewards of success, the pressure on the children to do as well as their parents, the tight-knit family that seems to have few social ties outside their bonds to one another: these are traits frequently found in upwardly mobile blacks. More-over, a number of small touches convey a sense of black ethnicity, including the African art that dec-orates the house, the way Bill sometimes falls into a black walk or style of dancing, even the fact that when he cooks for the family he decides to prepare Trinidadian food.

At the same time, it is definitely true that *The Cosby Show* is light-years away from *The Jeffer-sons, Good Times,* or *Sanford and Son.* On those shows, being black was turned into a comic rou-tine: Fred Sanford holding his chest and moaning, "It's the big one," J. J. rolling his eyes and saying, "Dynomite!" and George Jefferson call-ing white people "honkies" when he gets mad. But on *The Cosby Show,* being black is just an ordinary circumstance of life, like wearing glasses or having blond hair. It's not viewed as being comic, it's not viewed as being a problem, it's not viewed as conflicting with the larger culture.

Bill told one journalist that he did the new series because he had something to say. Executive pro-ducer Marcy Carsey explained what it was. "What Bill wanted to communicate is what he communi-cates in his monologues: 'I'm getting through the day, you're getting through the day, and there is a certain common ground among all of us who raise children, so let's look at it and find the humor in it.' " And he really does mean all of us, black and white, rich and poor, successes and failures. It is what Bill Cosby's idea of integration always has been and always will be: human beings sharing common emotions that arise from common human situations.

Chapter Twelve

Bill Cosby Is Certainly Himself These Days

I don't usually look back and regret, or try to figure out how it could have been. I look to the future.

If I died tomorrow, I'd like people to think of me as a man who had a lot of potential and who never got to use all of it.

SEVERAL YEARS AGO, Bill Cosby told an interviewer, "I know it's hard to keep pushing yourself into different areas, but you have to if you want to be around in a few years. In this business, if you stand still, you disappear!"

That philosophy has kept Bill constantly in search of new challenges. These days, he makes all the decisions about his career by himself, turning only to Camille for advice and moral support. He devotes himself to his career as matter-of-factly as any businessman would to his enterprise. He says, "A lot of people in show business leave off the word 'business,' and through the years I have taken into consideration that it's a serious, serious business. If it is handled properly, it is run no differently than Ford Motor Company or the way a doctor handles his business. First there is a talent that is salable. That's the product. Then there are the problems of improving and smoothing out the product so you can get it out to the public. This is done through rehearsals and with the thoughts and creativity that go into it, which may come from the product or from someone else. Now you have a business with a product to sell, and any man running a big corporation is not going to just watch dollars coming in, he's also going to watch the dollars going out. The problem is, most of us come from a low economic background where money is used just to pay bills. We are stunned when we realize that we can make a lot of money. We have no idea how the system works that is going to pay us so much money, so we leave off the most important part—protecting that money. Entertainers should believe in themselves—not only in their talent, but in having the ability to learn about business.''

Bill has learned to trust himself, and now he handles his own financial and career decisions. Among his investment interests are low-power television stations around the country. In partnership with Dr. J (Julius Erving, the basketball star), he negotiated to buy the New York Coca-Cola bottling plant from its parent company. And he has shown himself to be a shrewd handler of his own product. Marilyn Beck reported that in 1982, when Vegas hotels began pressing entertainers to take less money for their appearances there because of a drastic slump in business, Bill Cosby held firm. He said, "I'm proud of my drawing record—it's up there with the best of them. I would never ask more than I'm worth, but it's not fair to get less than I'm worth." When he sold his new series to NBC, he held out not just for an appropriate level of compensation, but also for the conditions that he felt were necessary to enable him to do his best, such as a convenient shooting location and artistic control of the show.

But for Bill, one of the best things about making all his own decisions is that it gives him the chance to take on any challenge that intrigues him, whether or not it is likely to pay immediate financial rewards. For example, he got himself booked into L. A.'s Whiskey à Go Go as a singer rather than a comic and went on to cut several vocal records, singing with a backup group. *Newsweek* commented, "When old Silver Throat sang, it was less a disappointment than an irrelevance, even though the notes came out more slivered than silvered." In fact, Bill's interest in music is long-standing. He likes to bang on the drums (he says it's because they are the only instrument you can play without knowing how to read music), and "some of his best friends" are musicians.

His special interest is the blues. In 1981, he acted as a combination host and impresario for a concert at Carnegie Hall that was part of the Kool Jazz Festival. As the *New York Post*'s Richard Sudhalter explained it, "Bill Cosby brought what appears to have been a pet fantasy to Carnegie

Hall. . . . He called it 'Present Company Included.' It involved teaming singer-guitarist B. B. King with a band of compatible souls—in this case organist Jimmy Smith, tenor saxophonist Arnett Cobb, cornetist Nat Adderly, and drummer Mickey Roker— and letting them and himself enjoy the result. And enjoy it they did, as Cosby wandered on and off, contributing asides, partial monologues.''

Bill also valued his freedom to choose to appear on shows that couldn't pay his usual big fees but brought some other reward. For example, he signed to do a regular five-minute segment on *Captain Kangaroo* that was designed to teach vocabulary, verbal skills, social awareness, and visual perception. It was aimed at preschoolers and reinforced through the use of booklets published by *Weekly Reader*. These segments began airing in 1980, and just recently they were collected on videocassettes so they could be a permanent educational tool.

Another of Bill's gambles was the making of a film of his performance in concert. It was first released in a limited-run engagement in big-city theaters and was then turned into a videocassette. Few comics would take the risk of presenting nearly two hours of their material to anything other than a live audience, and in fact, even the reviewers who liked the film commented on the problem of its length. But it represented an effort to find a way to extend the market of Bill's ''product,'' to reach the people who used to buy comedy albums but apparently do so no more. It may well be a precursor of more successful attempts to come.

On the business side of his career decisions, Bill's greatest success has probably been his work as a spokesperson in a number of well-known commercials for such products as Ford, Del Monte, Jell-O, and Coke. All of his commercials have been long-running, and the advertisers believe they have sold the product well. The keynote of Bill's commercials is warmth. He is often selling things that children like, and he is seen talking to children about why they like it. The rapport between the star and the real kids is palpable. Tom Carson, in the *Village Voice*, suggested an interesting interpretation of the Cosby persona in commercials: "In his routines about childhood, for instance, or his Jell-O commercials, he doesn't condescend explicitly; instead, he condescends implicitly—to you, the viewer—about his presumed superior intimacy with children. But what are you going to say—'I hate that man for how well he gets along with five-year-olds'? In his other jobs as a pitchman, he's never been used in the way most people defined as outsiders—or, for that matter, most comedians—get used in commercials: to impart some connotation of irreverence or wacky individuality to a product. Instead, he's the man in control—he knows what we all like, and his wry, self-assured one-upmanship is there only to tell us that his brand is above the competitive fray. Every product he endorses becomes, in his person, a monopoly."

Carson's analysis, although negative in some aspects, points up the reasons why Bill Cosby is such a comforting and comfortable presence. He radiates a sense of being in charge, of knowing what's best for us all. Like a good teacher, he's interested in our activities, but he still seems just a bit above it all. And, of course, he also communicates a sense of mature adult stability. We know that he is a nice guy, a reliable guy, someone who practices what he preaches. This sense of stability allows him to handle some fairly daring material without raising any eyebrows. For example, in his monologues, he often talks about his irritation with his wife and her negative attitude toward matters having to do with the children; he claims he longs for a remote control that can change her real-life channel. He also talks about his disappointment that his first child was a girl and jokes about having considered smothering her and trying again. In the hands of some comics—Richard Pryor, for example—such material would make the audience uncomfortable because they would be aware of the hostility that lurks behind such jokes (and that knowledge would be reinforced by the gossip they have heard about his private life). But Bill Cosby can get away with such material because the audience understands instinctively that he loves his wife and children and would never willingly harm them. He's just expressing every man's annoyance with the way the world works.

Critic John Leonard summed it up: "Tirelessly, Cosby reassures. Love goes on, even if it's black. Children get his message, especially if they're white. Cosby isn't dangerous, in the way that Pryor and

Eddie Murphy are, with their secret thoughts and seethings. Cosby bears no resentment; he won't hurt; he affirms; he's adorable. He won't talk to us like Jesse Jackson, and he won't be killed like Martin Luther King. He sells Jell-O.''

What does the future hold for Bill Cosby fans? Happily, there's much more of his unique blend of comedy, warmth, and assurance to come. *The Cosby Show* is likely to become a permanent fixture on the NBC schedule; with the ratings it is currently drawing, it will probably remain on the air until Bill gets too weary of it to go on. And there will be more live appearances at his favorite clubs in Tahoe and Vegas. Bill never likes to get too far away from the live audiences and the stand-up comedy that have been his inspiration and the fertile breeding ground for his best material.

A special treat in store for us all is the book Bill is currently working on. He has signed a contract with Doubleday to write a book on fatherhood. A blend of comedy and practical advice, the book will draw on his own experiences as a father as well as his educational background.

Perhaps the safest prediction to make about Bill Cosby and his future is that he will surprise us. He may appear at a ballet gala, reminiscing about his experience as a spear carrier in *Aïda*, as he did in the summer of 1984. Or he may be running in the masters division for a relay team, as he did in 1983. He might put on sneakers with his black tie and rappel down a Plaza Hotel stairwell, as he did in the fall of 1984 for an Outward Bound dinner

Bibliography

THE FOLLOWING MATERIALS were especially helpful and are also the source of otherwise unattributed quotes within the book.

Beck, Marilyn. Syndicated column, August 16, 1982.
———. Syndicated column, August 17, 1984.
Bennetts, Leslie. "Bill Cosby Begins Taping NBC Series." *The New York Times*, August 6, 1984.
Blandford, Linda. "Why Cosby Never Gets a White Girl." *Sunday Times of London*, June 30, 1968.
Carcaterra, Lorenzo. "Cosby: Rapport with Kids Helps." *New York Daily News*, March 19, 1980.
Cohen, Joel. *Cool Cos: The Story of Bill Cosby*. New York: Scholastic Book Services, 1969.
Davidson, Bill. " 'I Must Be Doing Something Right.' " *McCall's*, April 1985.
deRoos, Robert. "The Spy Who Came In for the Gold." *TV Guide*, February 3, 1973.

deSherbinen, Polly. "Bill Cosby, Student and Educator."
     Christian Science Monitor, May 20, 1974.

DiPetto, Adam. "Laughing on the Outside Too." *New
     York Sunday News.* October 25, 1970.

Fury, Kathleen. "Witness the Humors of Bill Cosby."
     TV Guide, October 13, 1984.

Gardella, Kay. "Teacher Role for Cosby Plumbs Hu-
     man Behavior." *New York Daily News.* August
     12, 1969.

————. "The Wacky World of Bill Cosby." *New York
     Sunday News,* August 13, 1972.

Glenn, Larry. "Bill Cosby: The Clown as Straight
     Man." *Tuesday Magazine,* October 1965.

Haddad-Garcia, George. "Bill Cosby: Being a Daddy."
     Black Stars, February 1980.

Hale, Wanda. "Cosby and Culp Return as Super-Losers."
     New York Sunday News, September 10, 1972.

Jennes, Gail. "That Doctorate After Bill Cosby's Name
     Is No Honorary Freebie." *People,* June 6, 1977.

Look magazine, unsigned article. "TV's Bright-Spoken
     Bill Cosby Does the Vegas Bit." May 30, 1967.

Morgan, Thomas B. " 'I Am Two People, Man.' "
     Life, April 11, 1969.

Newsweek, unsigned article. "Color Him Funny." Jan-
     uary 31, 1966.

Robinson, Louie. "Dr. Bill Cosby." *Ebony,* June
     1977.

Stang, Joanne. "The Case of the Scholarly 'Spy.' "
     The New York Times, October 17, 1965.

Sternig, Barbara. "Bill Cosby: Why My Show Is Hottest
     New TV Hit Ever." *National Enquirer,* April 2,
     1985.

Whitman, Arthur. "The Spy Who Knocked 'Em Cold."
     True: or, The Man's Magazine. January 1967.

Woods, Harold and Geraldine. *Bill Cosby: Making Amer-
     ica Laugh and Learn.* Minneapolis: Dillon Press,
     1983.

MORE BESTSELLERS FROM TOR